Hoberg's Atelier
HOLMESTRAND
Pladen opbevares for Efterbestilling.
INSTANTANEOUS PORTRAITS OF CHILDREN
A SUCCESSFUL SPECIALTY
Stevens
Art Studio
McVicker's Theatre Bldg.
CHICAGO.
DUPLICATES CAN BE HAD AT ANY TIME.
A SPECIALTY.
LANDSCAPE VIEWS TAKEN.
Artistic Photographer
A. W. Phipps
72½
WASHINGTON ST.
NEW CASTLE
PA.
Shew's
Photographic Art
Studio,
DUPLICATES CAN BE HAD AT ANY TIME
LIFE SIZE AND INSTANTANEOUS PHOTOGRAPHS
A SPECIALTY
523 KEARNY ST.
San Francisco,
Cal'a.
No.
Imperial Studio
PORTRAITS
724
MARKET ST.
San Francis
CA
Duplicates can be had at any time
PHOTOGRAPHERS
CHICAGO
NEGATIVES PRESERVED FOR FUTURE ORDERS
угол Соборный и Морской
домъ Утца
ATELIER
A. HARTMANN
INH. WILLIBALD HARTMANN
PHOTOGR. KUNSTANSTALT
GROSS-SCHÖNAU
AF880441

Now and Then

THE CABINET CARD PAINTINGS OF

Alex Gross

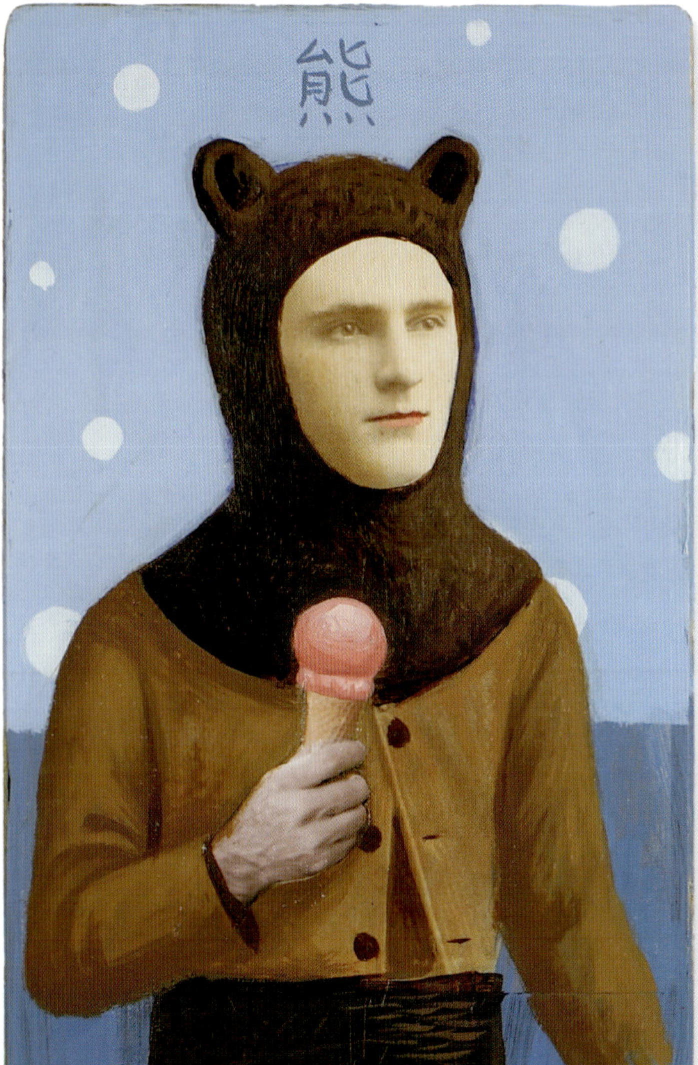

熊
gross

Now and Then

The Cabinet Card Paintings of

Alex Gross

Gingko Press

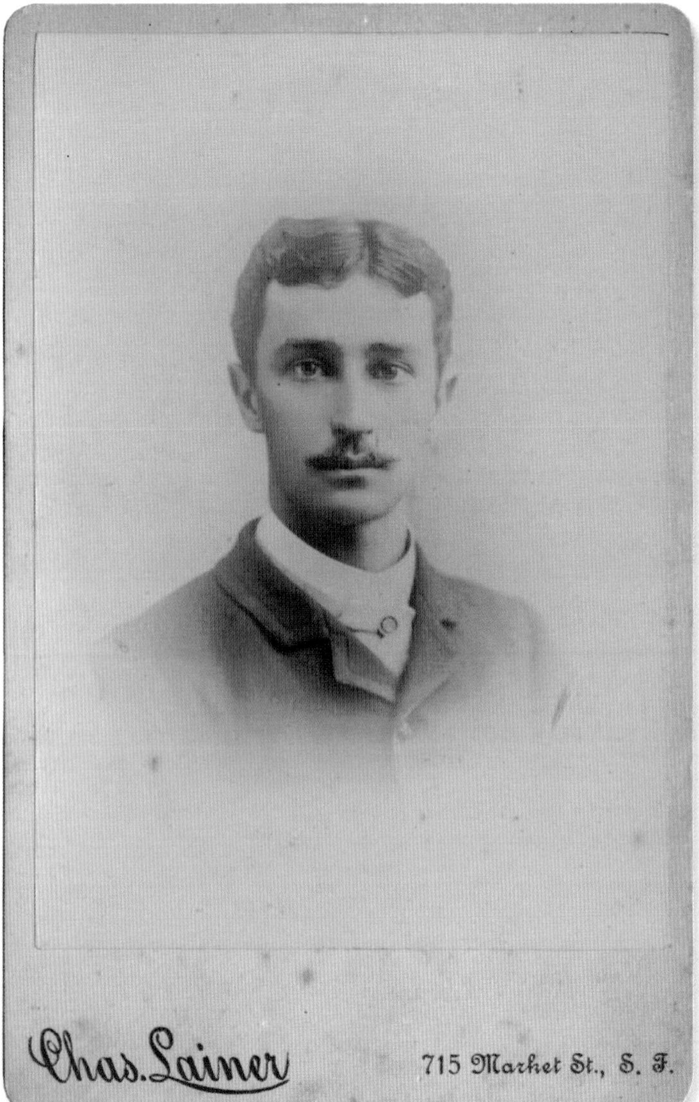
Chas. Lainer
715 Market St., S. F.

INTRODUCTION

I began collecting Cabinet Card photographs around twelve years ago. I first discovered them at antique stores and flea markets, and began assembling a small collection of cards that portrayed interesting and unique looking men and women. It astonished me to learn that these cards were well over one hundred years old (in most cases), yet very inexpensive. Cabinet Cards are early photographs which are mounted on heavy card stock. They were the common form of portrait photography in America from the 1860s through around 1910.

Some of the characters from these photographs began working their way into my paintings around this time. Usually I would redraw the person portrayed in another setting, add hands or a body, and place him or her into a whole new scene. Then, about four years ago, for a gallery exhibition, I had the idea of painting directly on some of the cards, instead of representing the people from them. I felt that the combination of a real antique photographic object with a modern, colorful paint job might make for some interesting artwork.

The 98 paintings in this book span a period of about four years, from 2008 to the present, and represent work done for three separate exhibitions. All of these pieces are mixed media paintings done directly upon real Cabinet Card Photographs. I use a combination of acrylic and oil paints as well as photo collage to make them. The first step is always to seal the photograph with a clear acrylic coat that will protect the image underneath it. From there, I simply have fun and experiment with different ideas. Many of the cards are inspired by characters that influenced me as a child, or even as an adult. Heroes and villains from comics, film, and television are all influences. Some cards are not representative of iconic figures, but are created from my imagination, or are inspired by something else entirely.

I followed a few simple guidelines in the process of creating these pieces. In the few cases where there was writing on the front of the card, I never painted over it (Franty Ferguson, page 84). When there was a name on the back of the card, I usually integrated it into the piece. Jacob Harden (p. 33), Lola (p. 85) , and Ed Cleall (p. 68) are all examples of this. And, most importantly, I always retained most of the person's face.

At the back of the book, I have included several images of the cards before they were "repurposed". I think it's interesting to see what the card looked like before I worked on it. Perhaps you can find which one is the alter ego of your favorite. Sometimes, you can get a feel for why I was inspired to make someone into a monkey, a monster, a superhero, or a circus performer.

— Alex Gross
February, 2012
www.alexgross.com

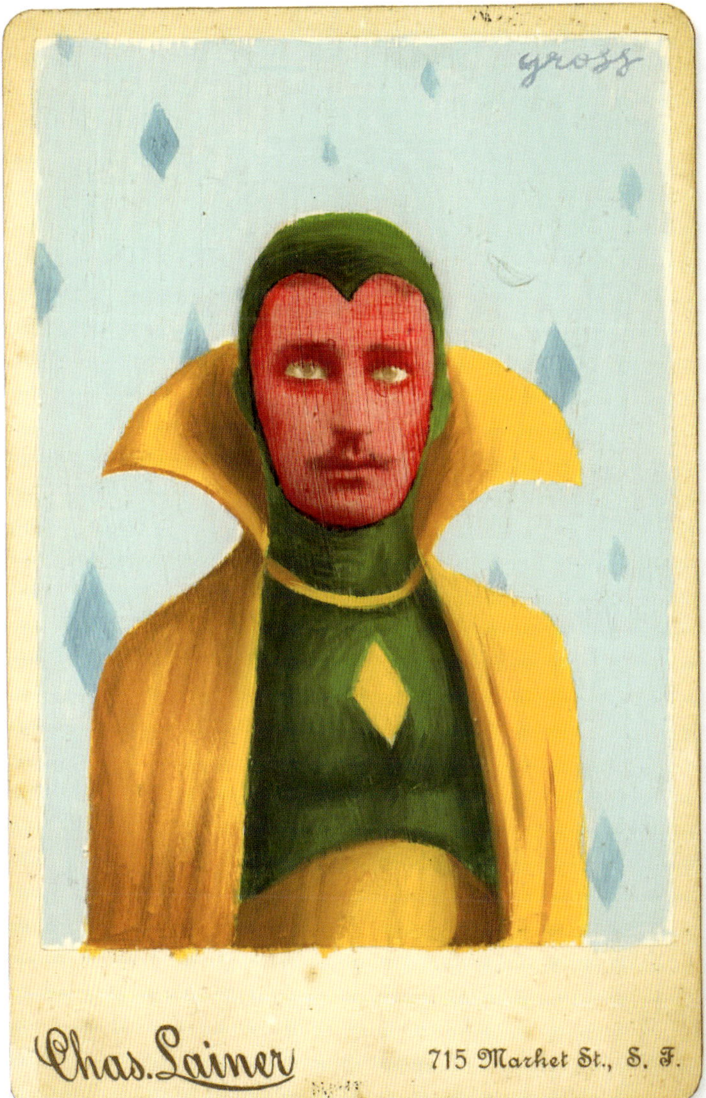
gross
Chas. Lainer
715 Market St., S. F.

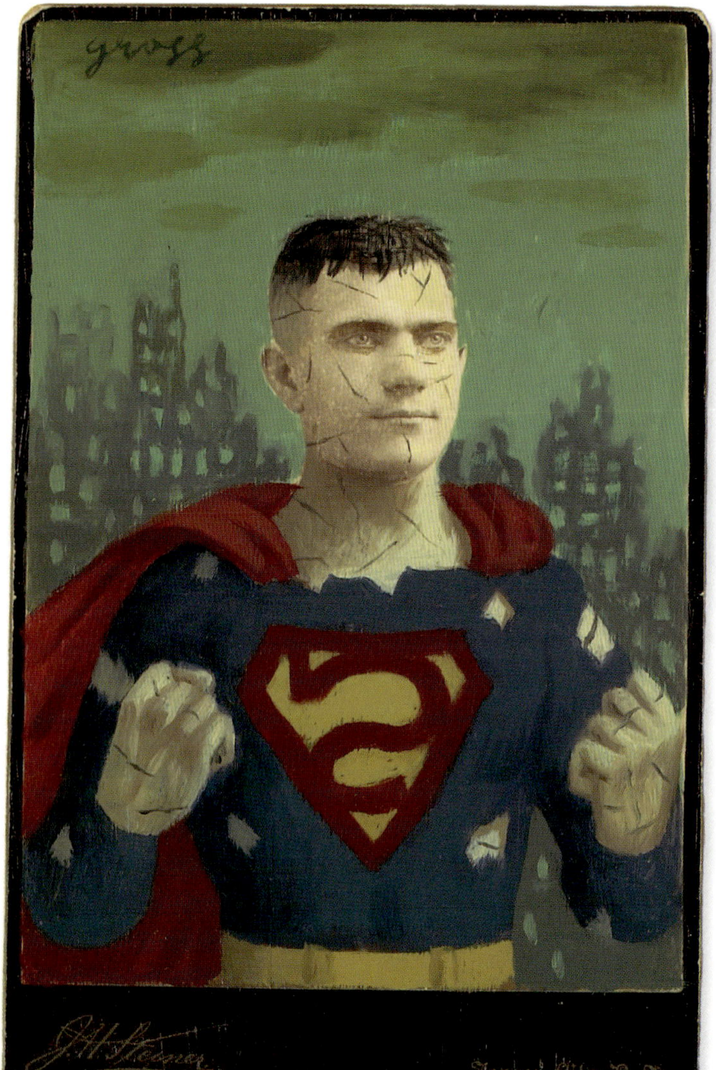
Jersey City, N. J.

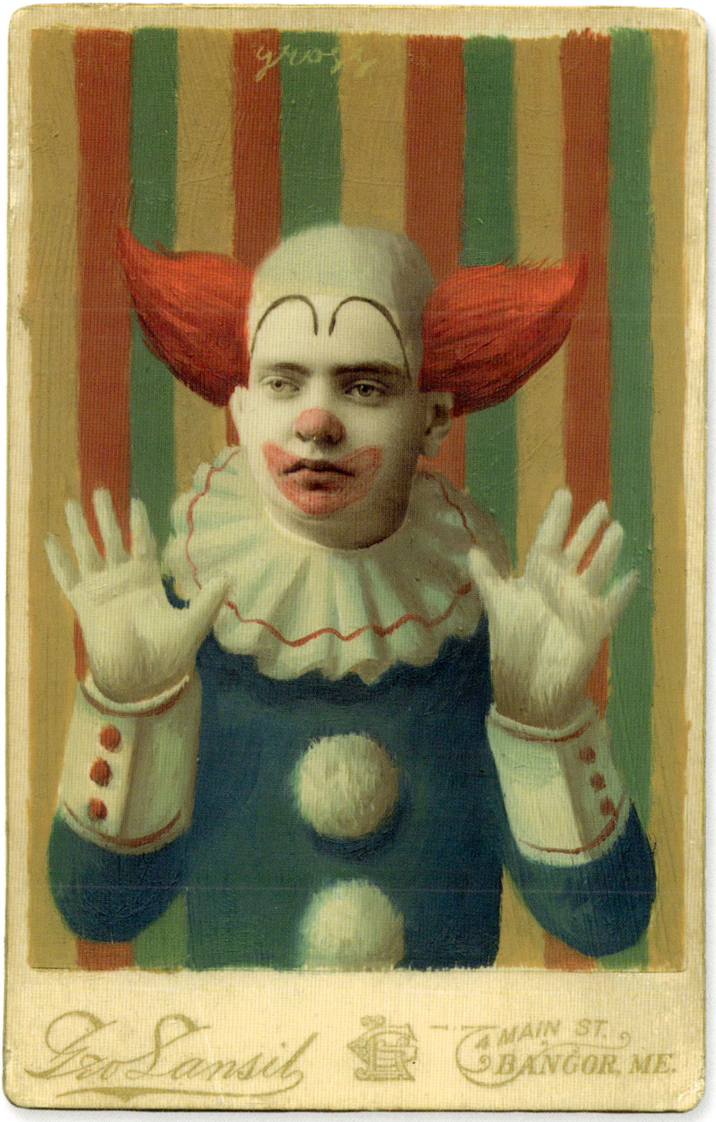
4 MAIN ST.
BANGOR, ME.

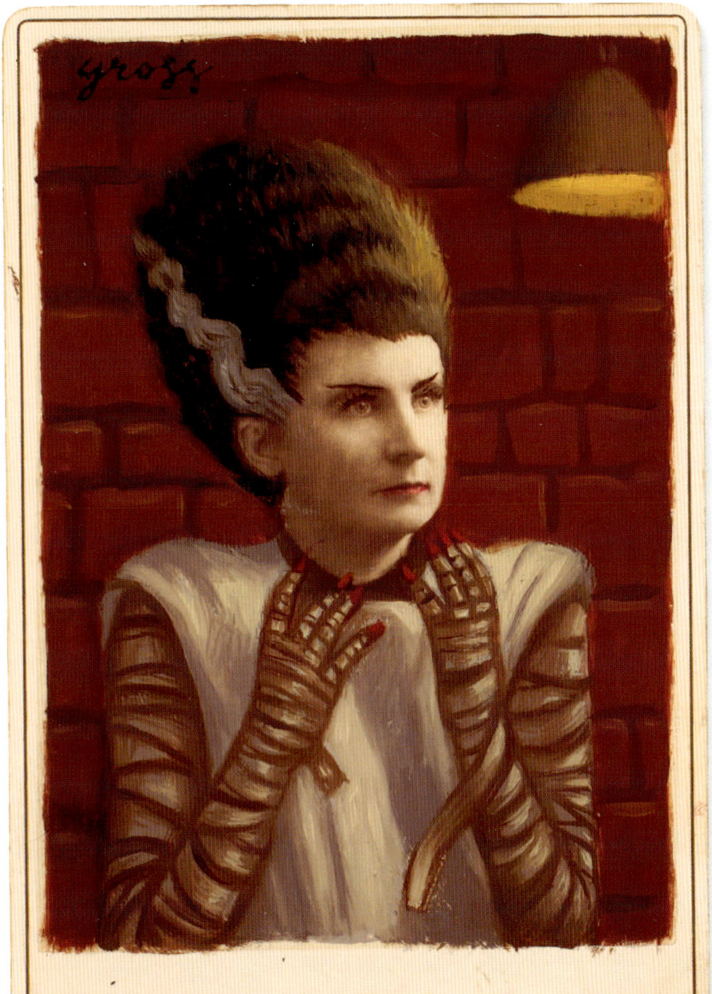
Reitmeyer
East Bridge & 2d St.
OSWEGO N.Y.

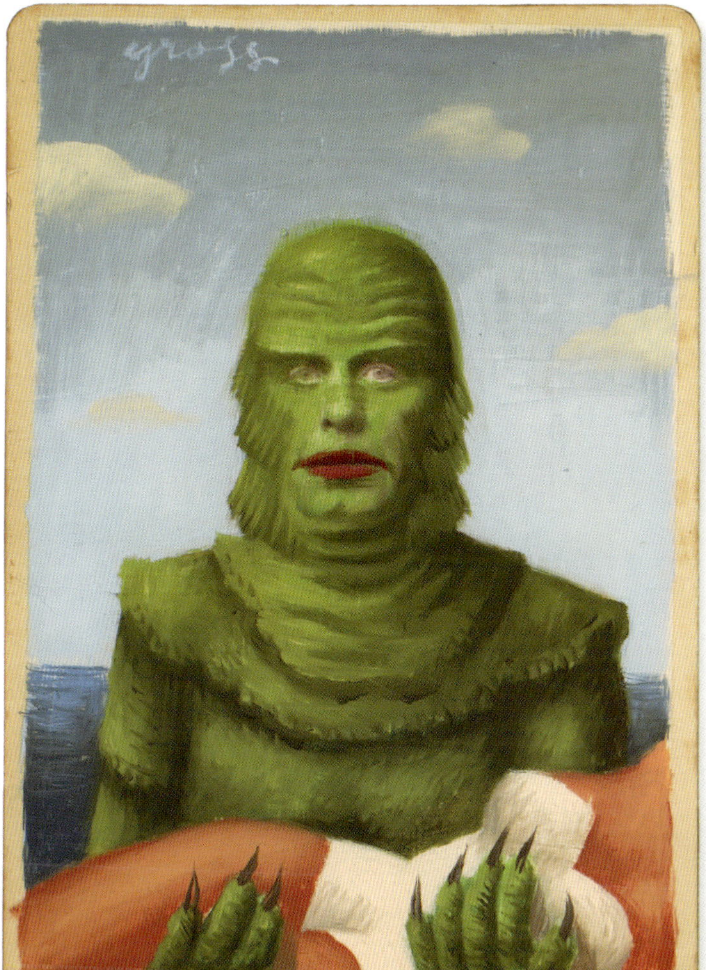
gross
J.G. Hucks.
25 Third St. S.F.
New York Gallery,

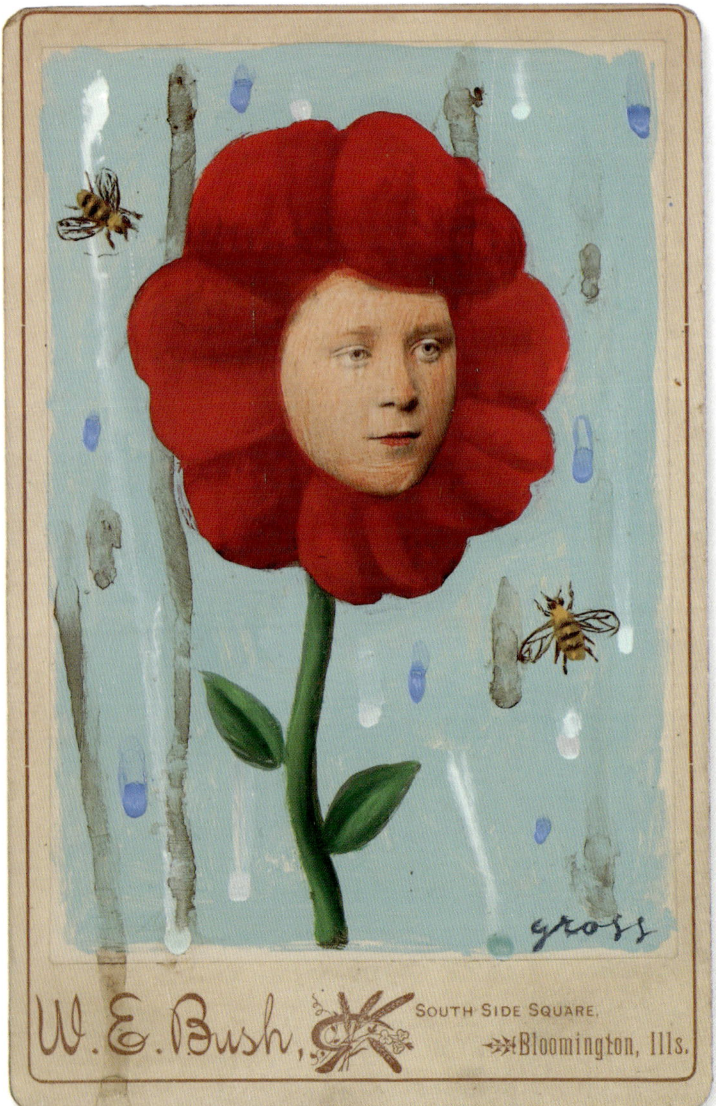
gross
W. E. Bush,
SOUTH SIDE SQUARE,
Bloomington, Ills.

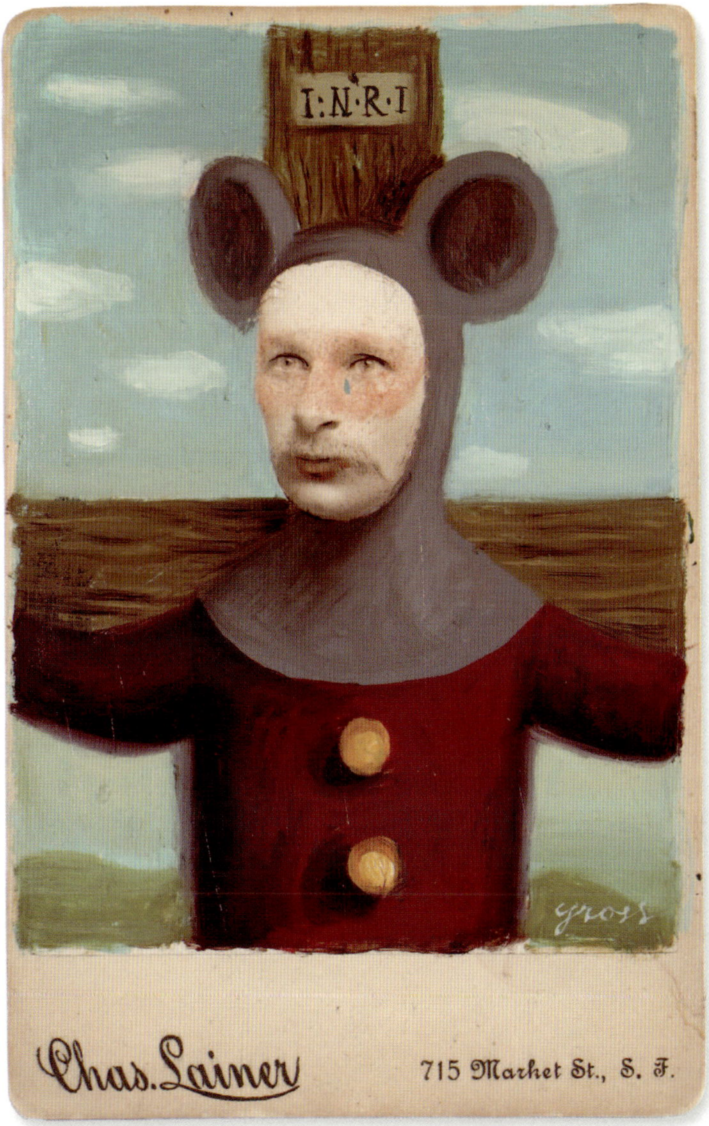
I.N.R.I
gross
Chas. Lainer
715 Market St., S. F.

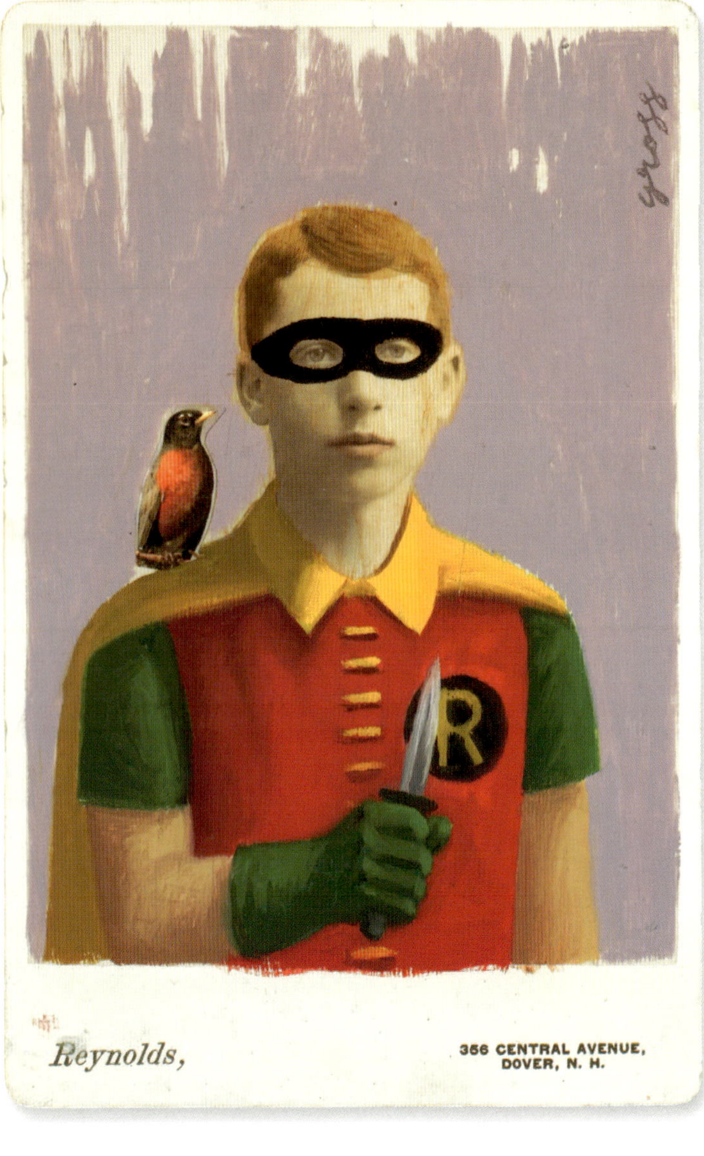
Gross
Reynolds,
356 CENTRAL AVENUE,
DOVER, N. H.

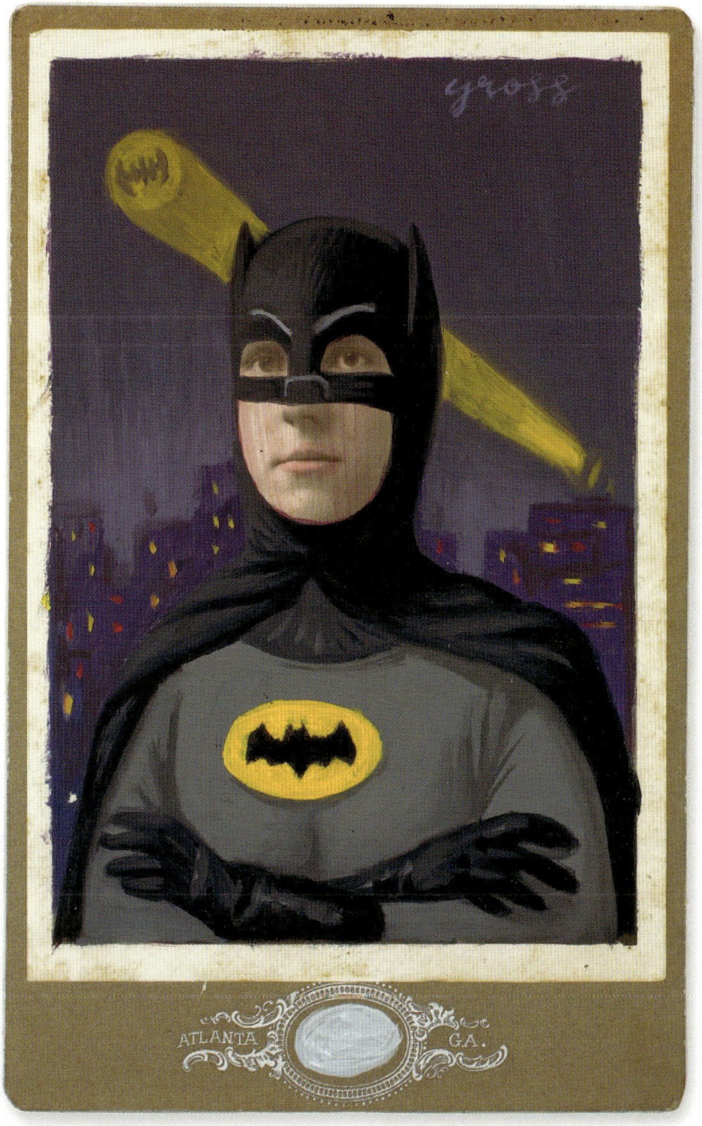
gross
ATLANTA
GA.

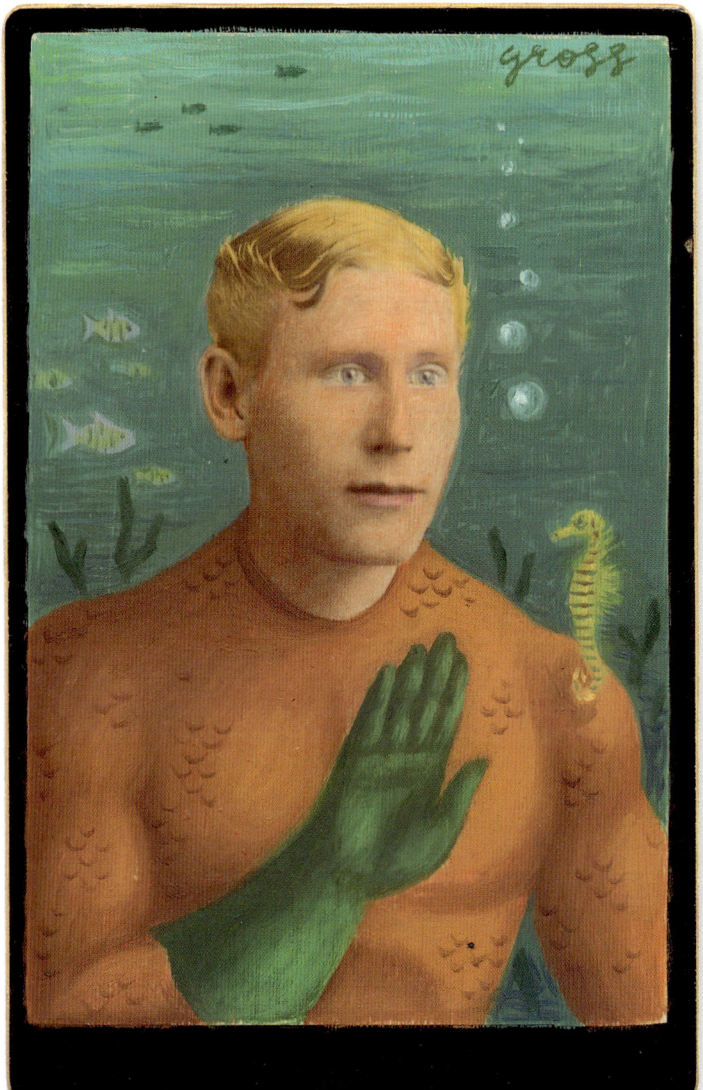
gross

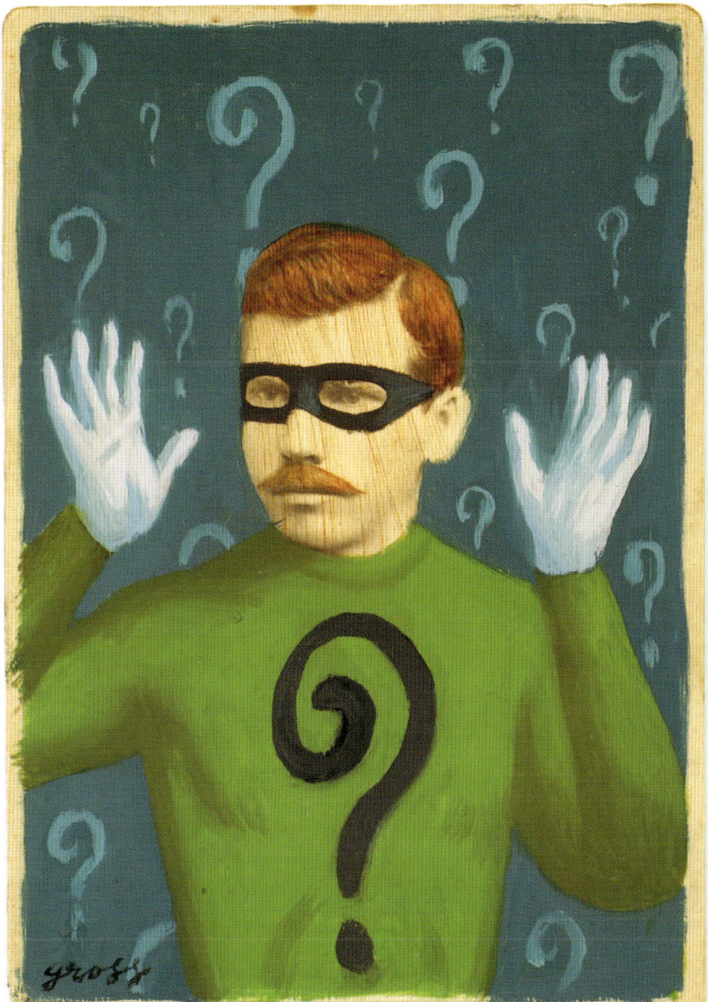
gross
DORÉ
GALLERY
1144
MARKET STREET S. F.

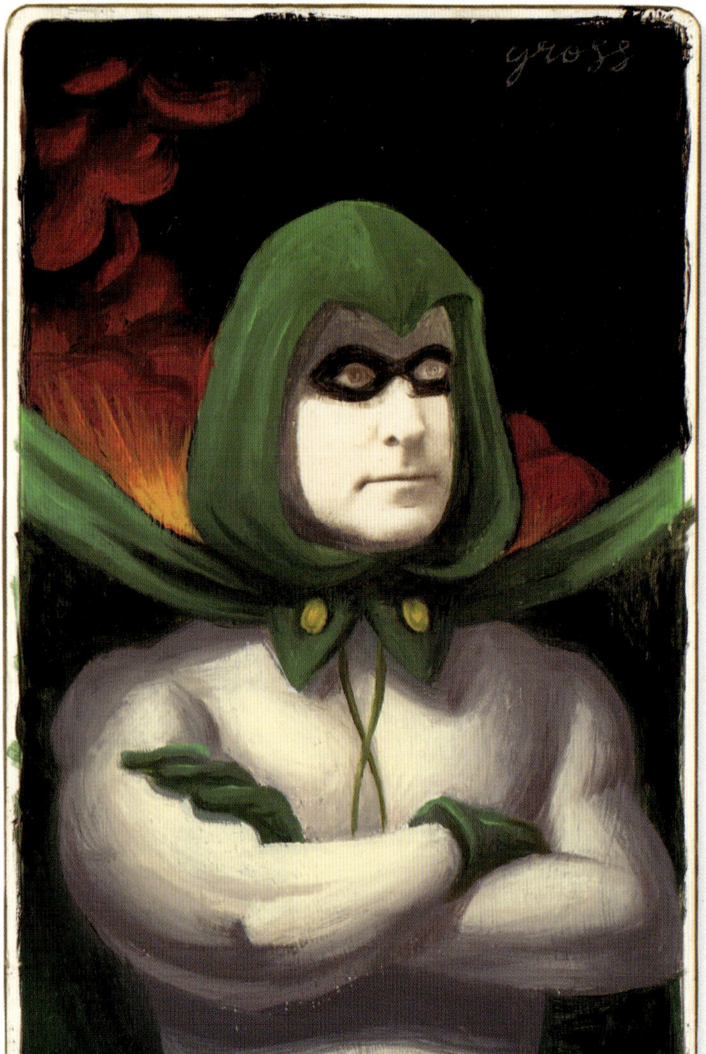
gross

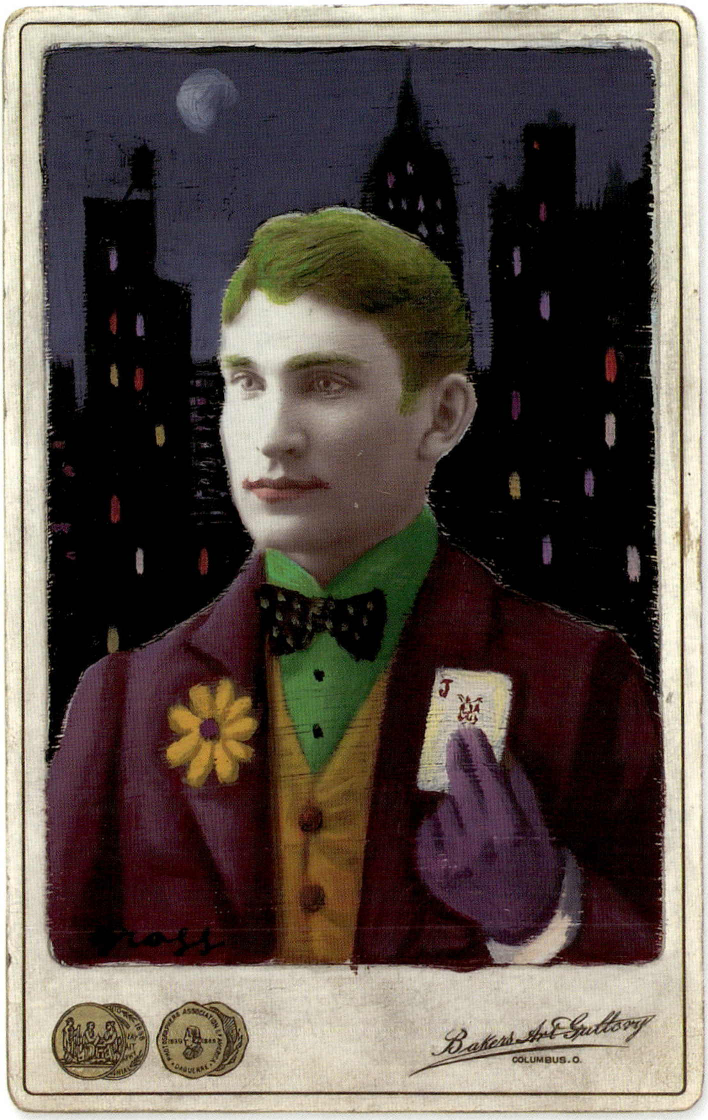
Bakers Art Gallery
COLUMBUS, O.

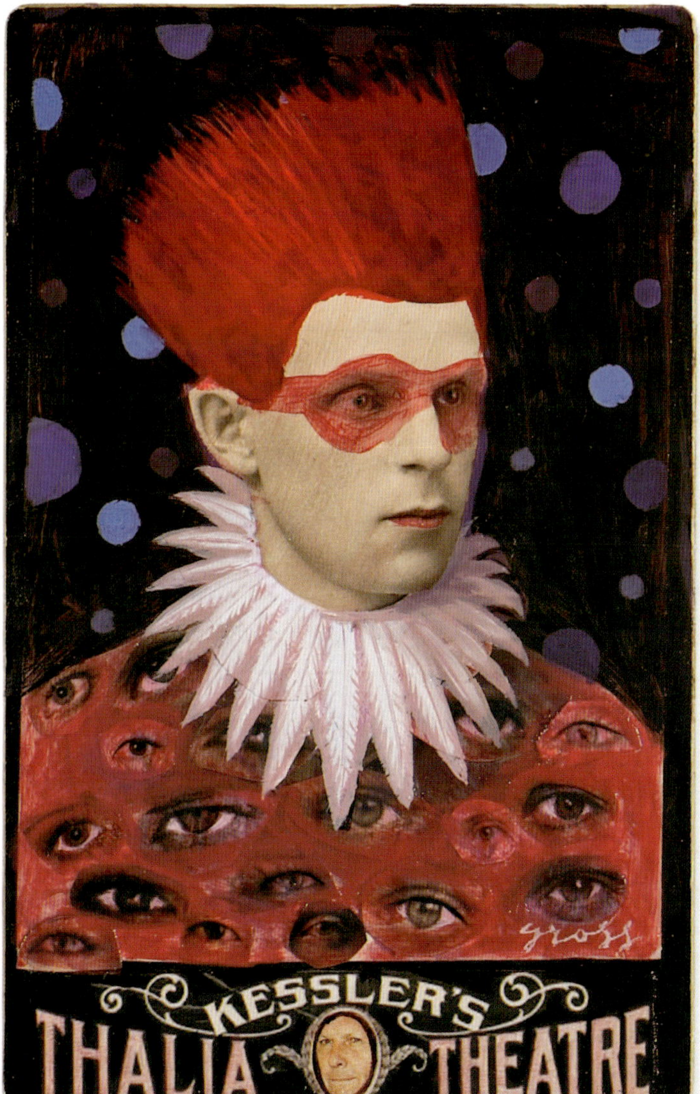
gross
KESSLER'S
THALIA THEATRE

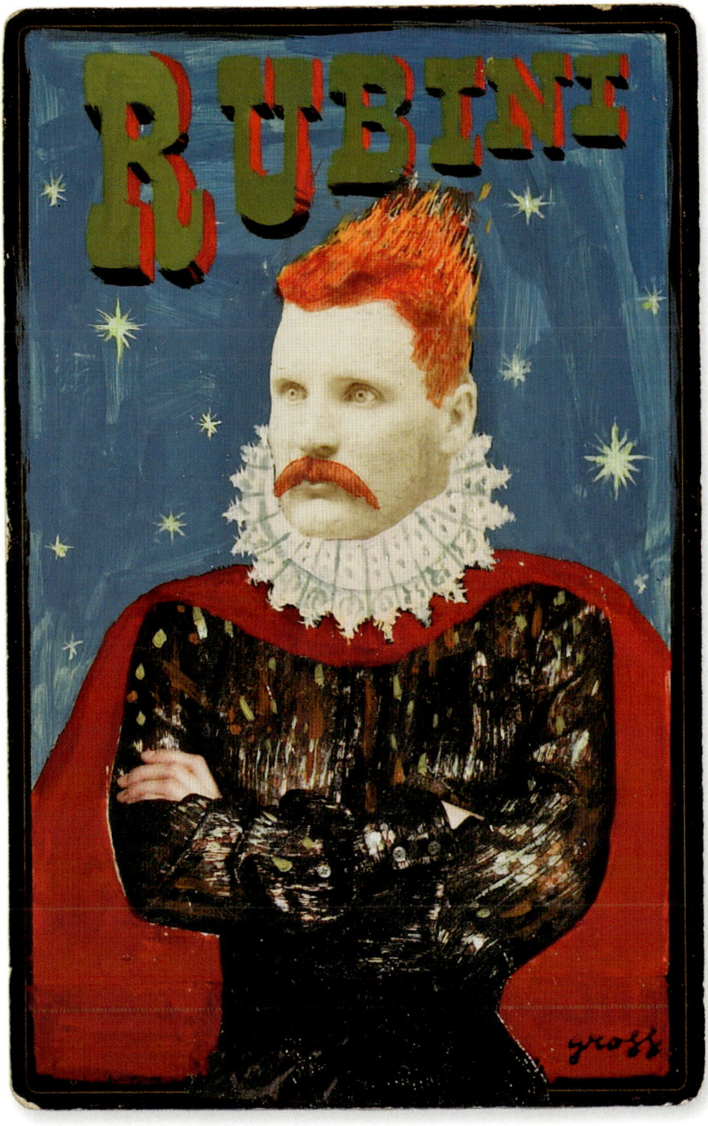
RUBINI
gross

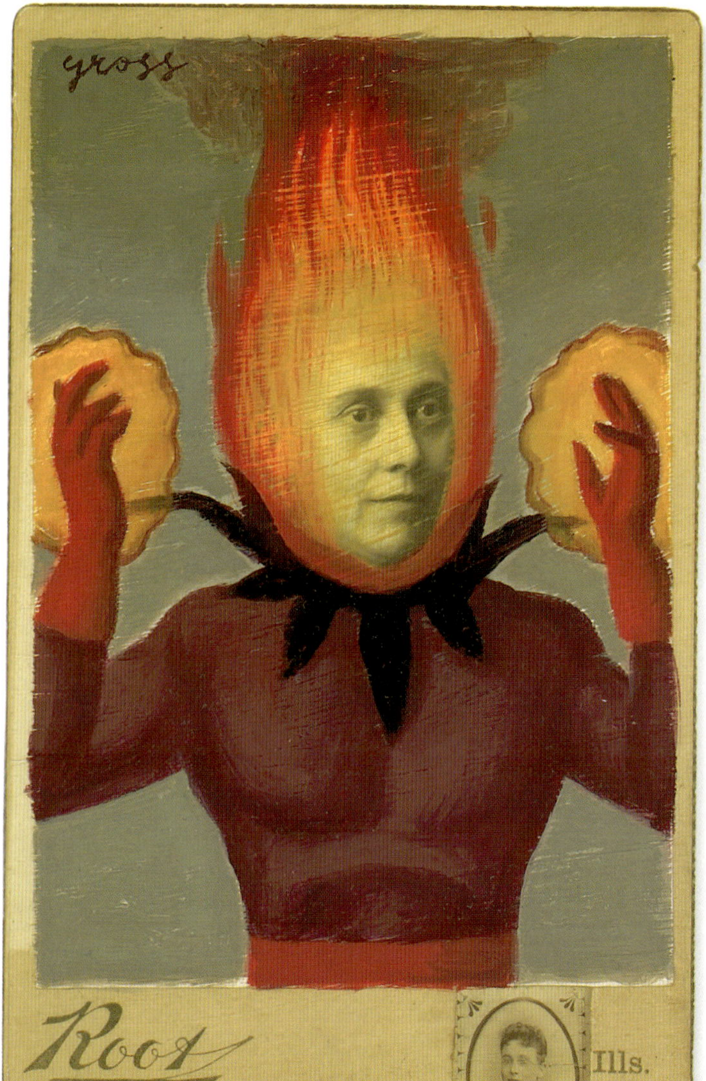
gross
Root
Ills.

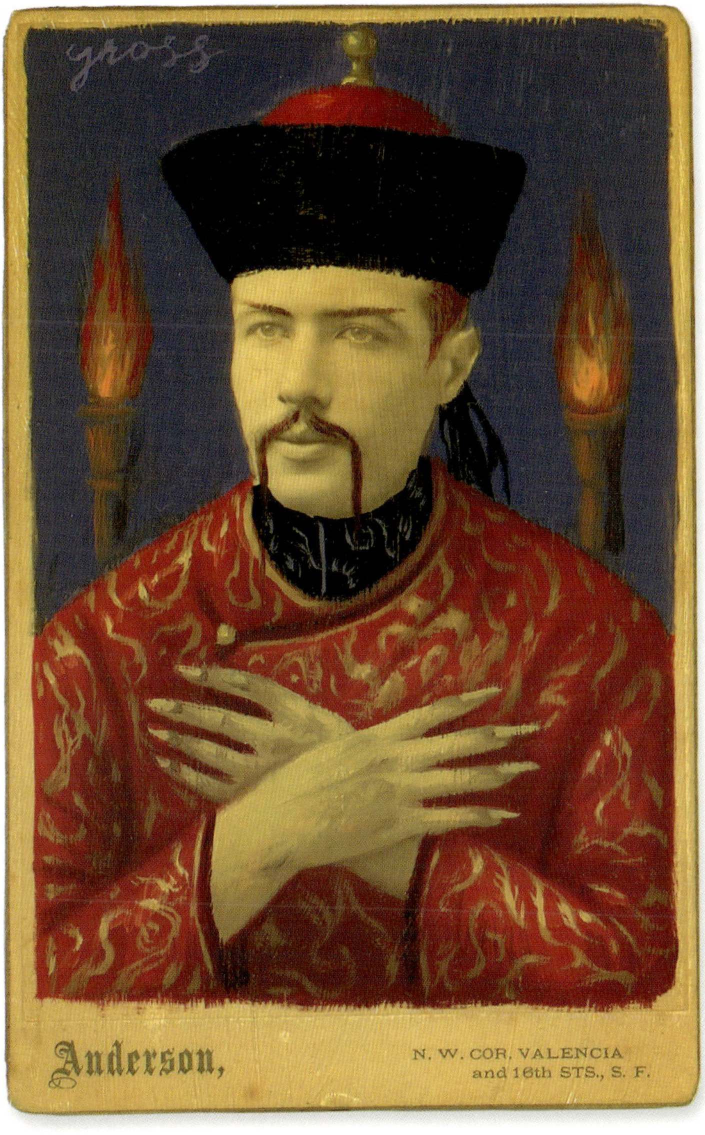
GROSS
Anderson,
N. W. COR. VALENCIA
and 16th STS., S. F.

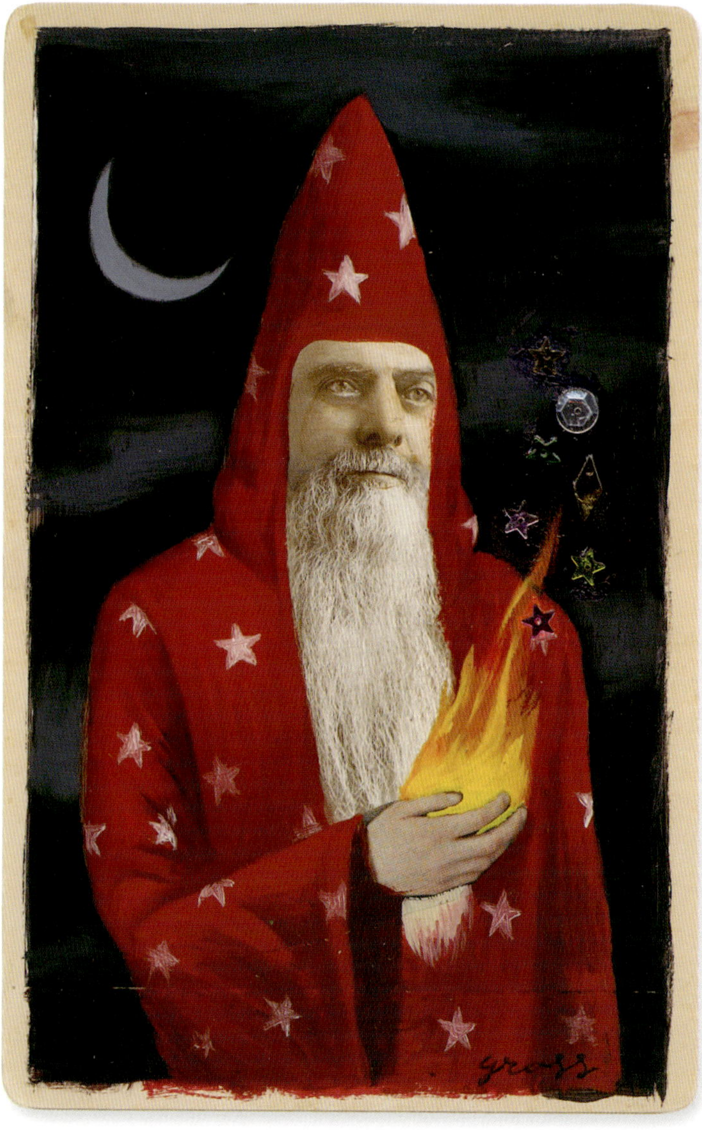

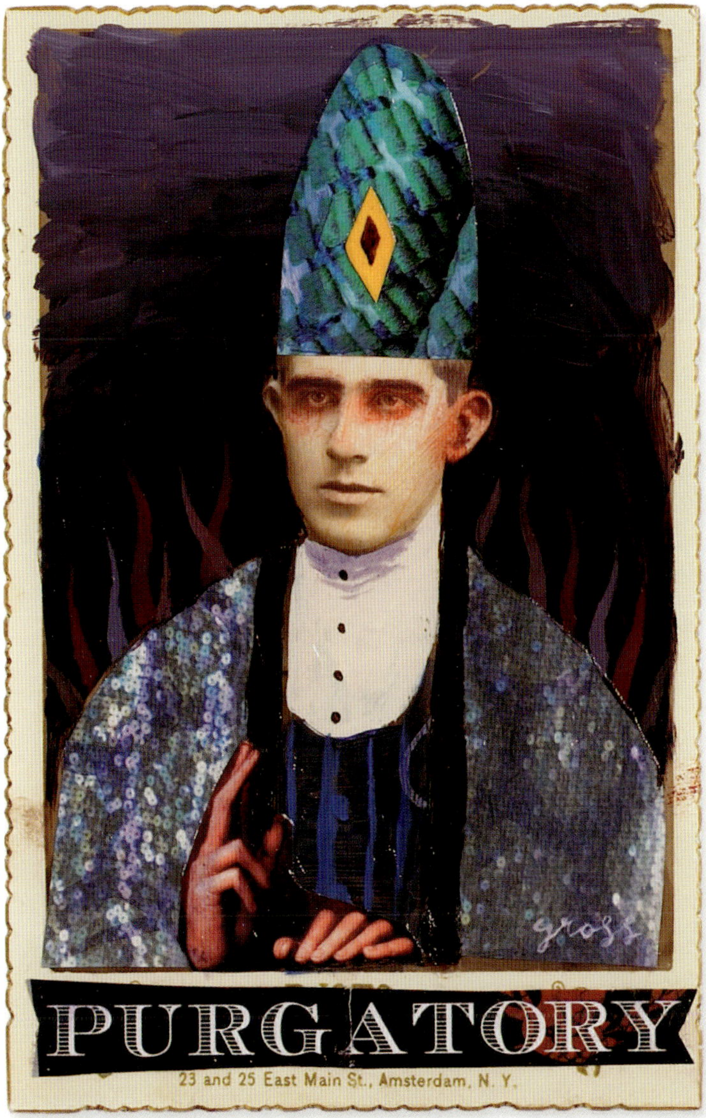
gross
PURGATORY
23 and 25 East Main St., Amsterdam, N. Y.

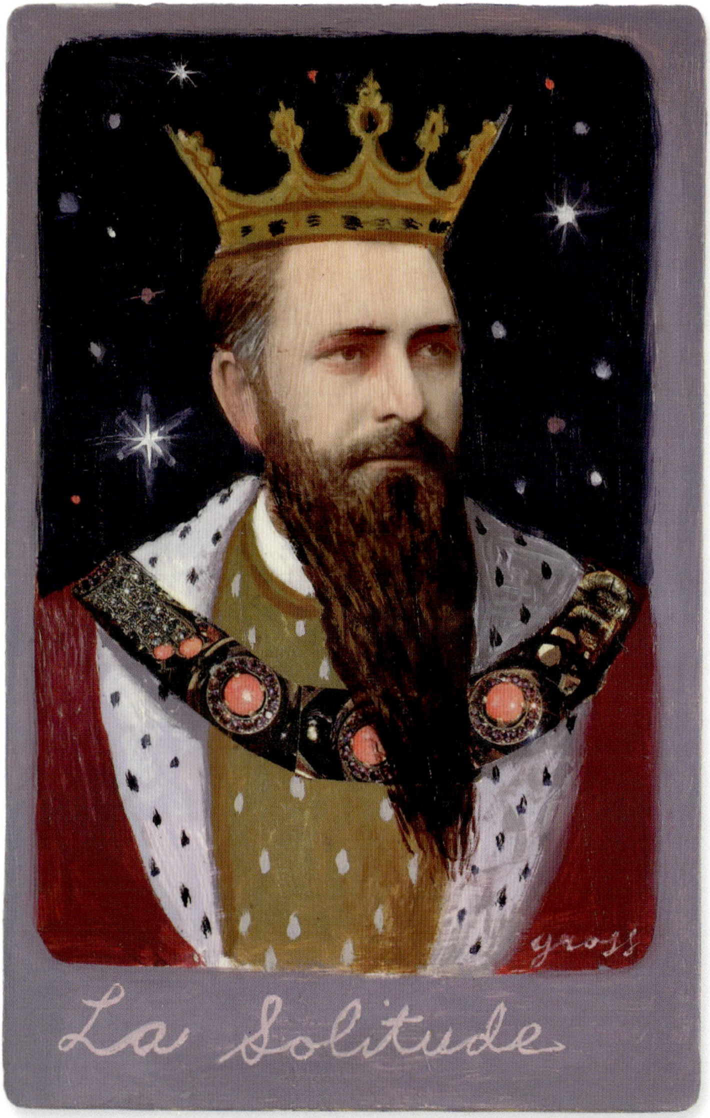
gross
La Solitude

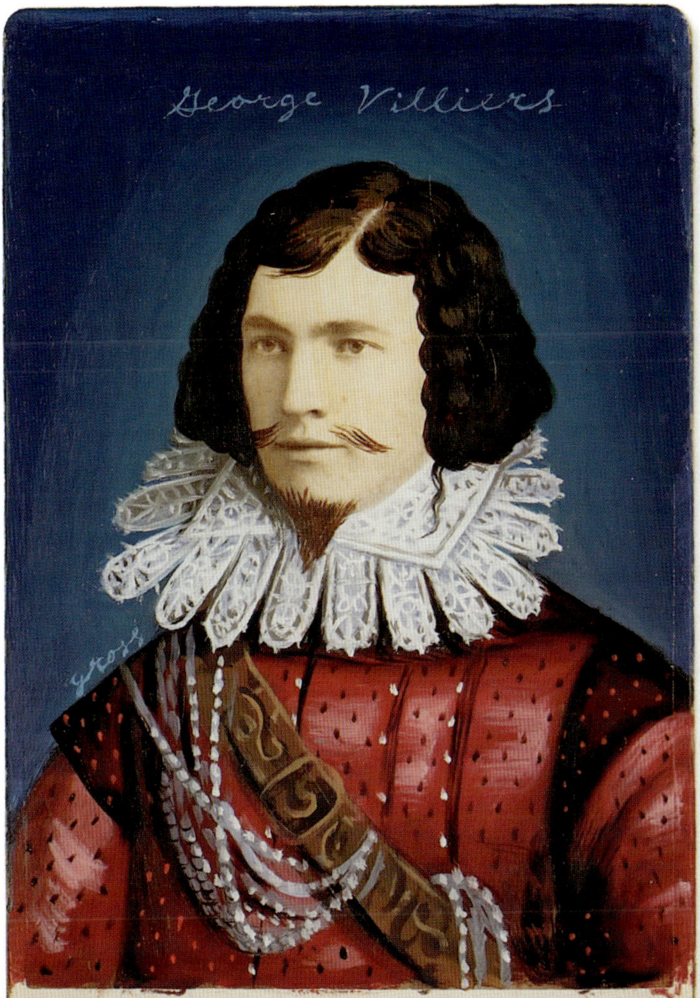
George Villiers
Gross
Camp.
Jamestown, N.Y.

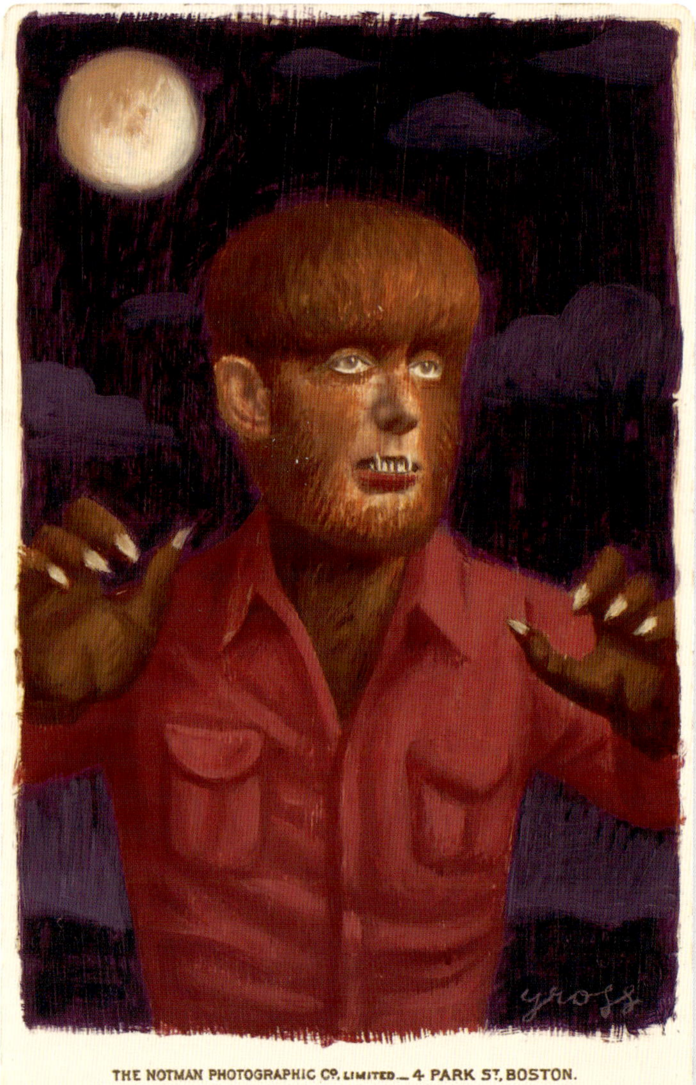
yross
THE NOTMAN PHOTOGRAPHIC Co. LIMITED — 4 PARK St. BOSTON.

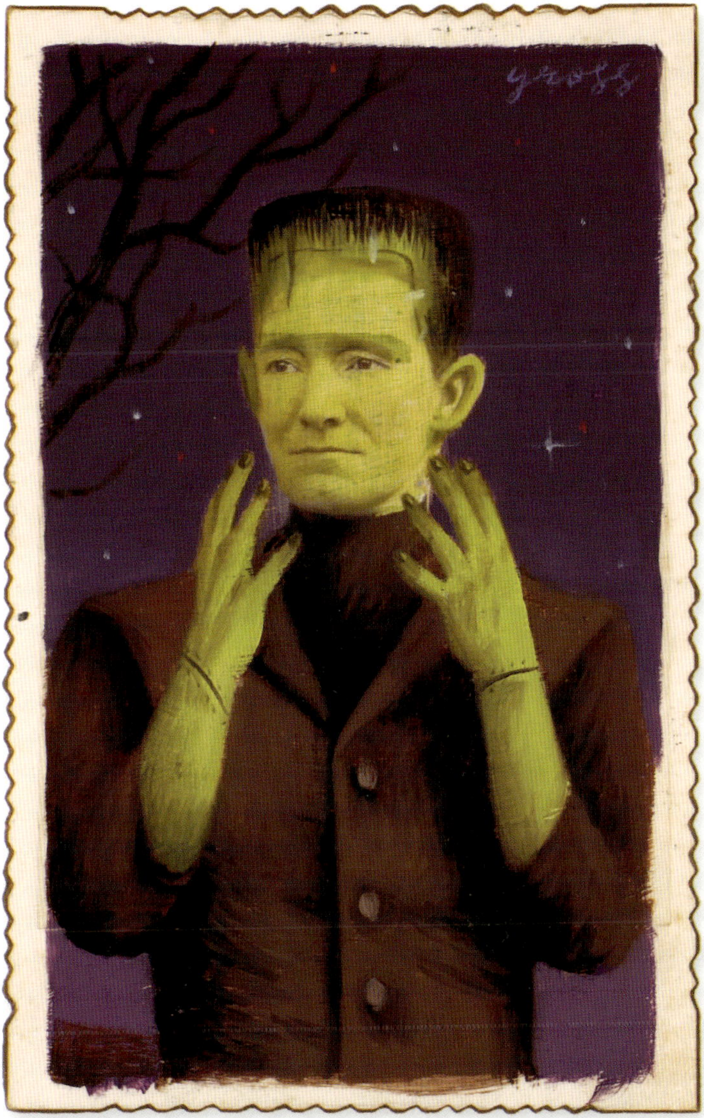

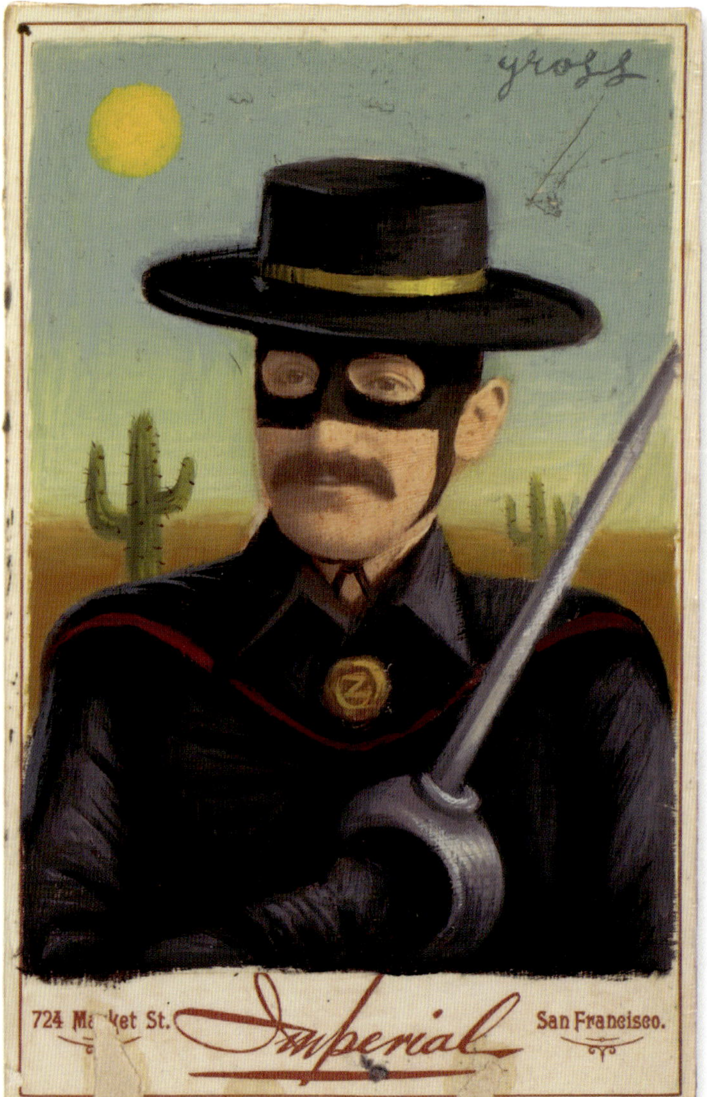
gross
724 Ma ket St.
Imperial
San Francisco.

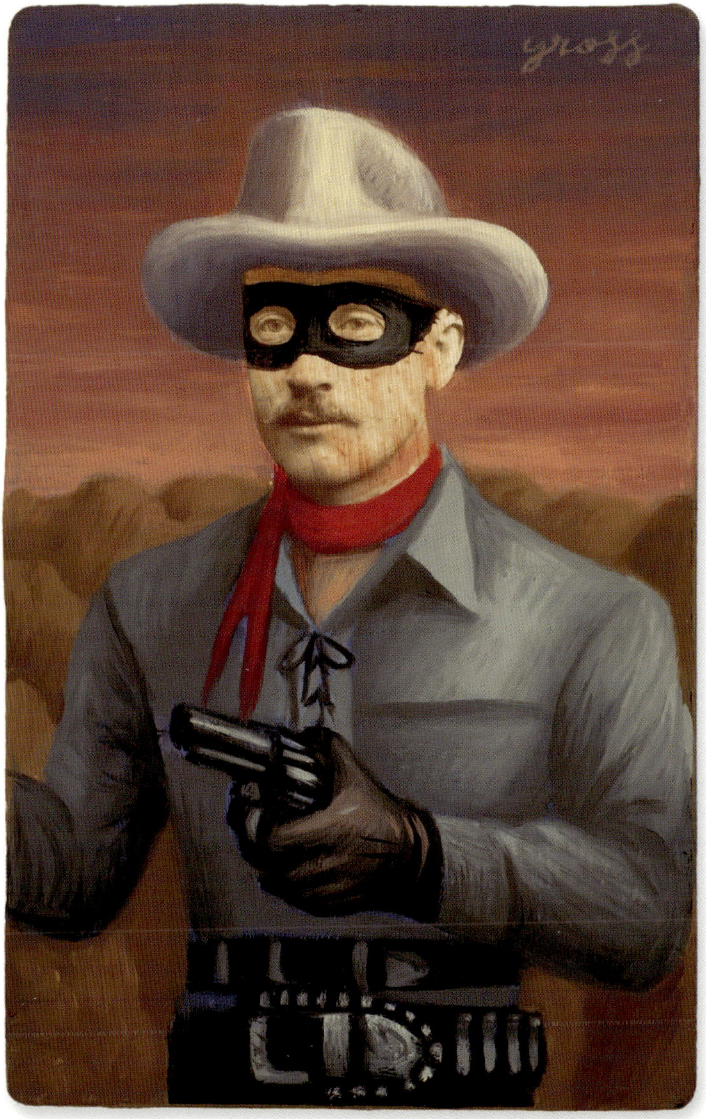
gross

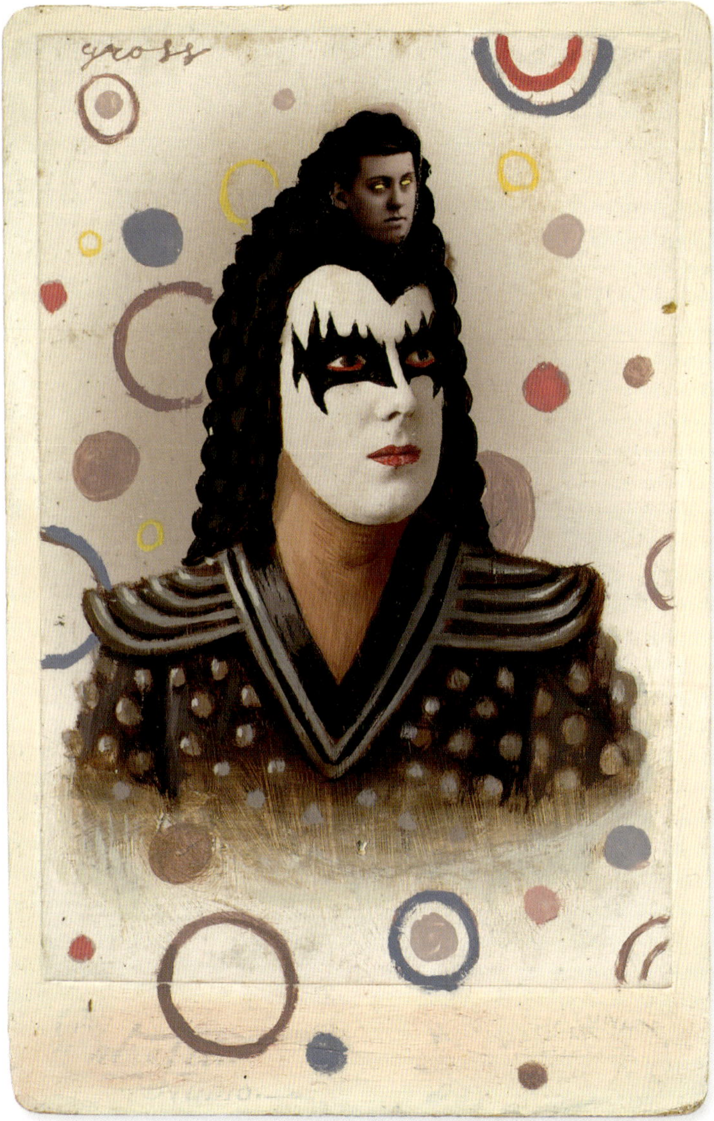
gross

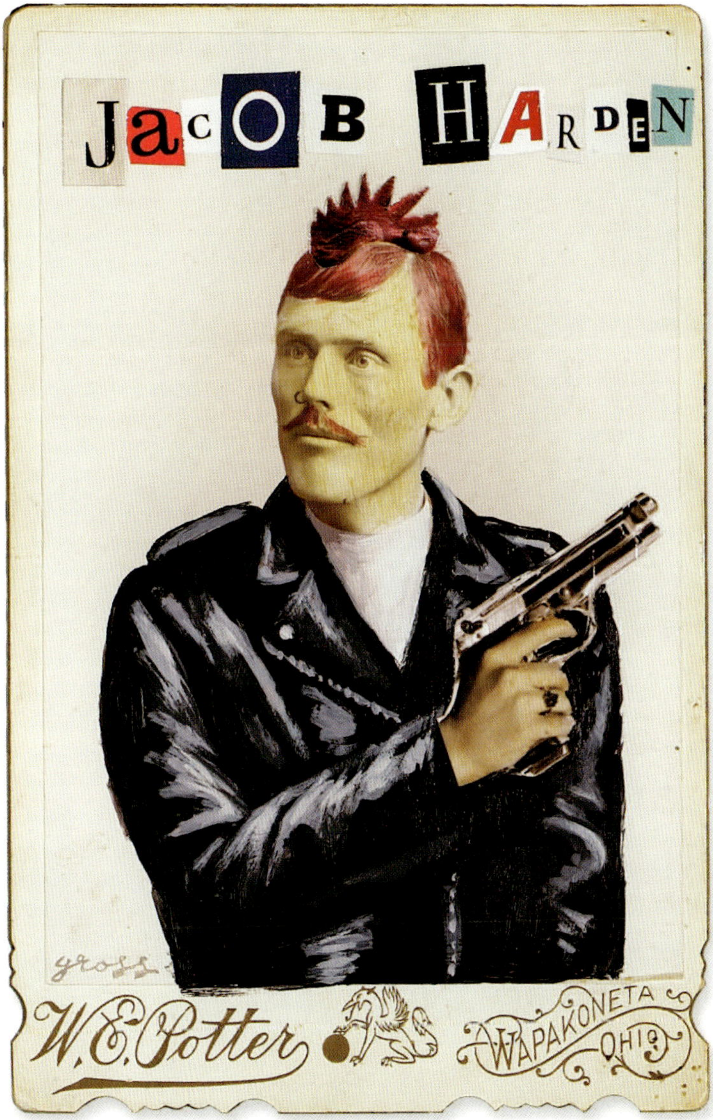
JACOB HARDEN
W. E. Potter
WAPAKONETA OHIO

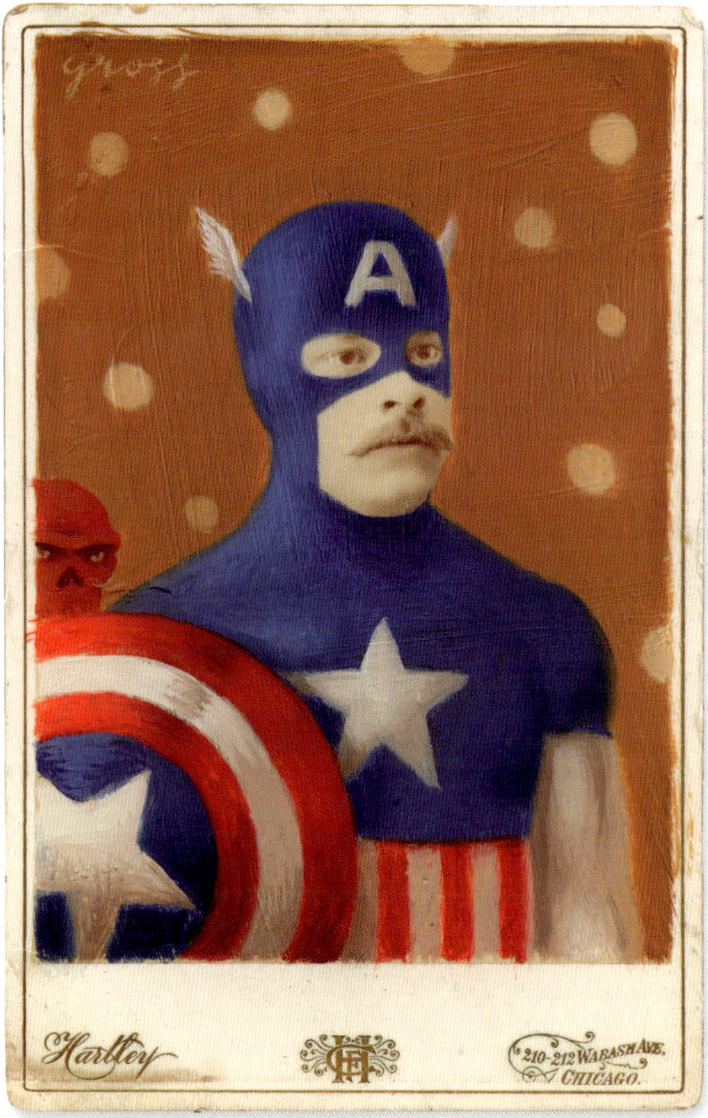
Hartley
210-212 WABASH AVE.
CHICAGO.

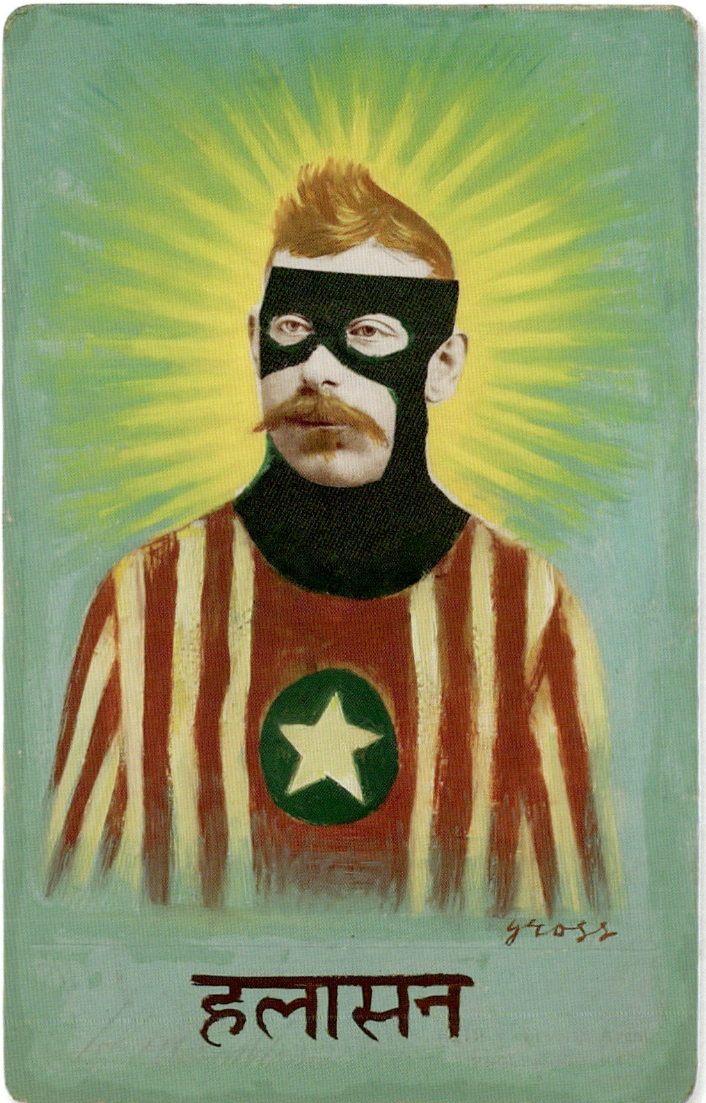
Gross
हलासन

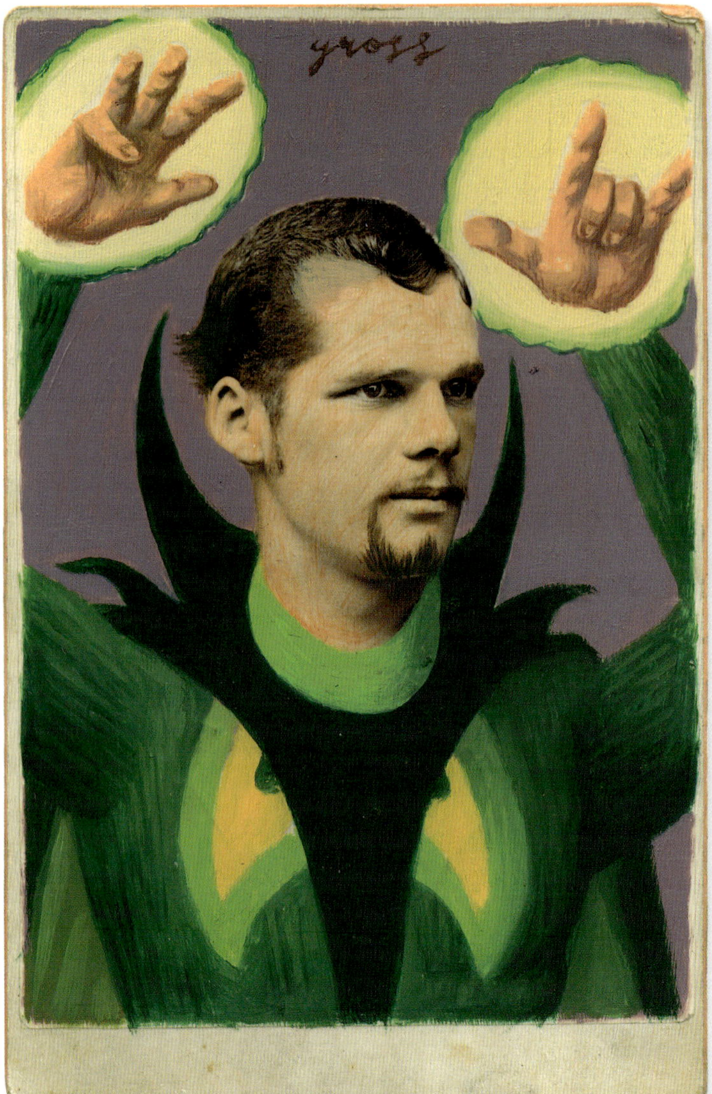
gross

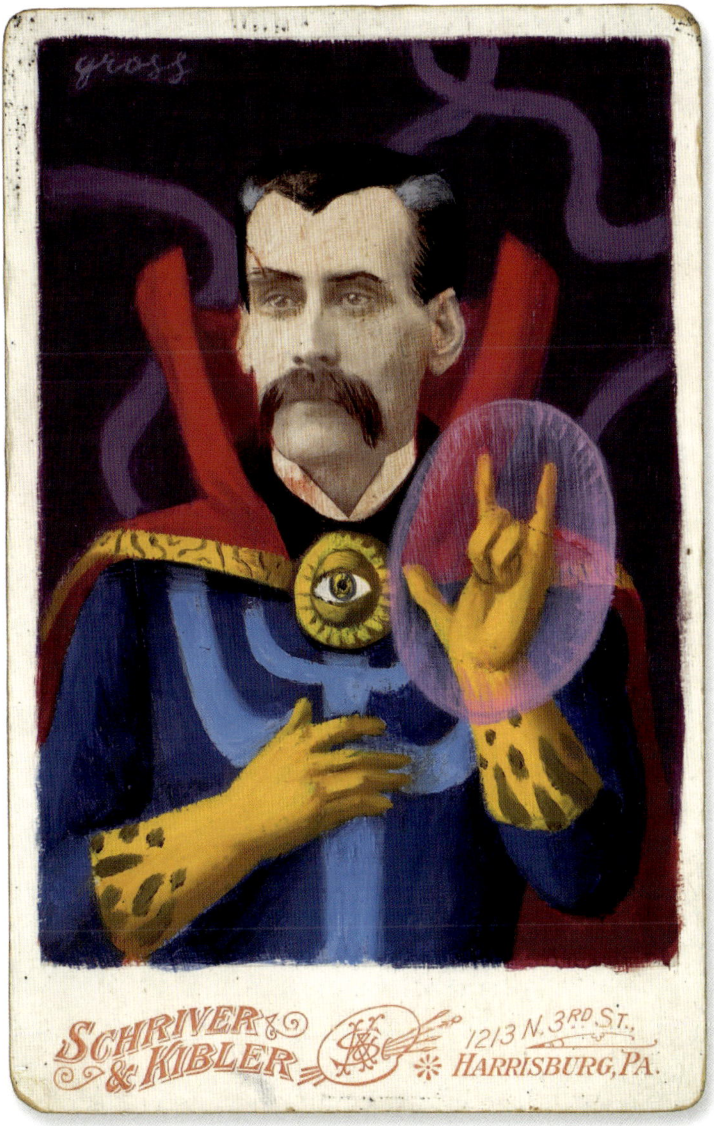
gross
SCHRIVER & KIBLER
1213 N. 3RD ST.,
HARRISBURG, PA.

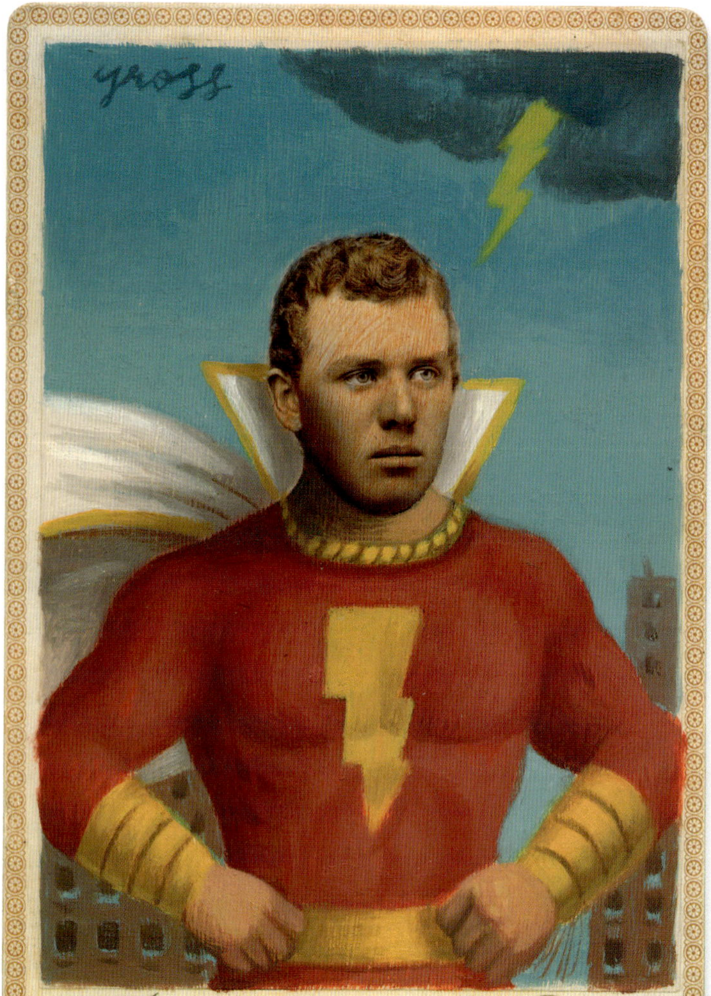
Gross
Fenner and Son
Superior Finish
Westfield, Wis.

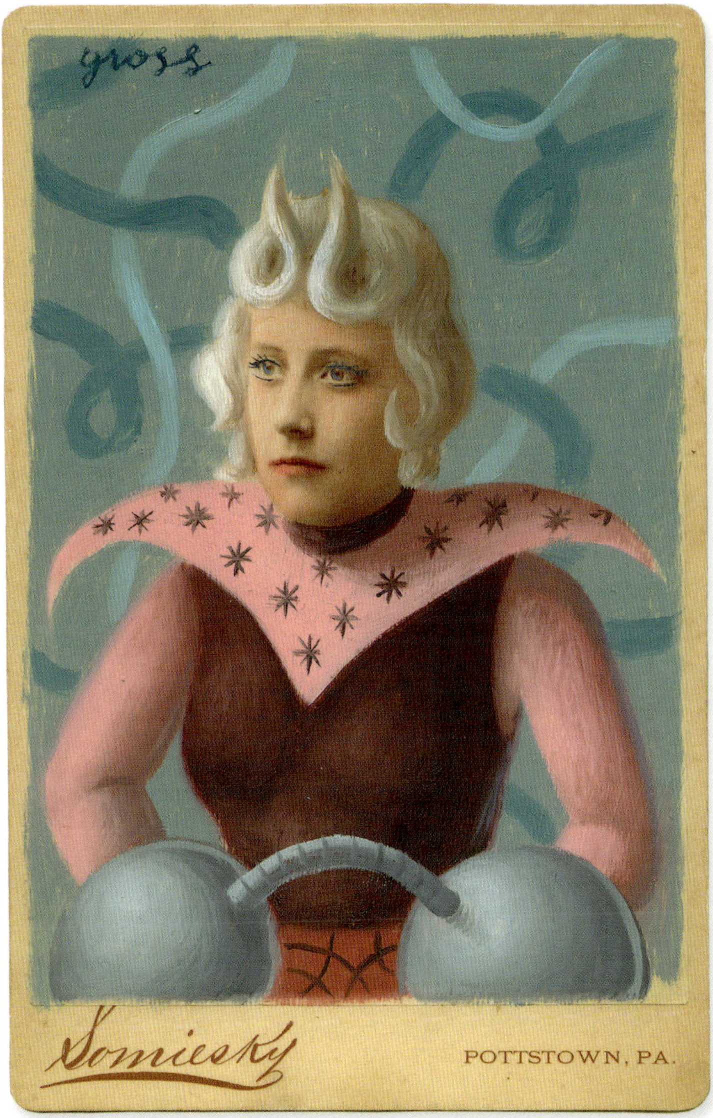
gross
Somiesky
POTTSTOWN, PA.

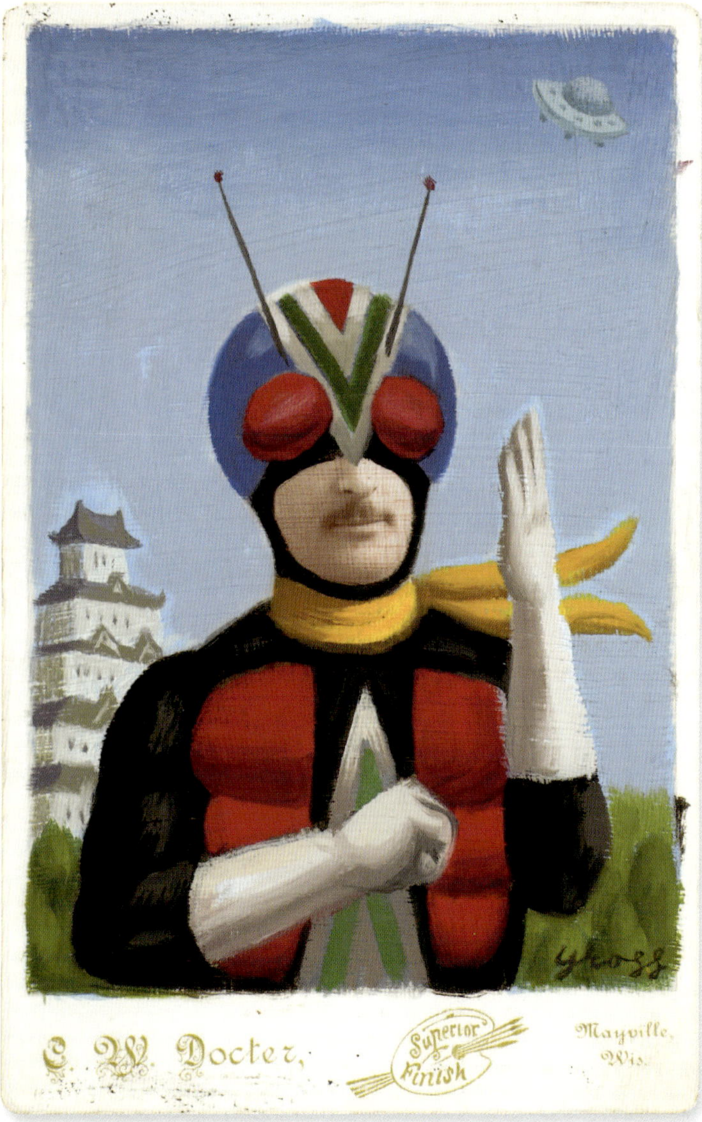
Ykoss
C. W. Docter,
Superior Finish
Mayville,
Wis.

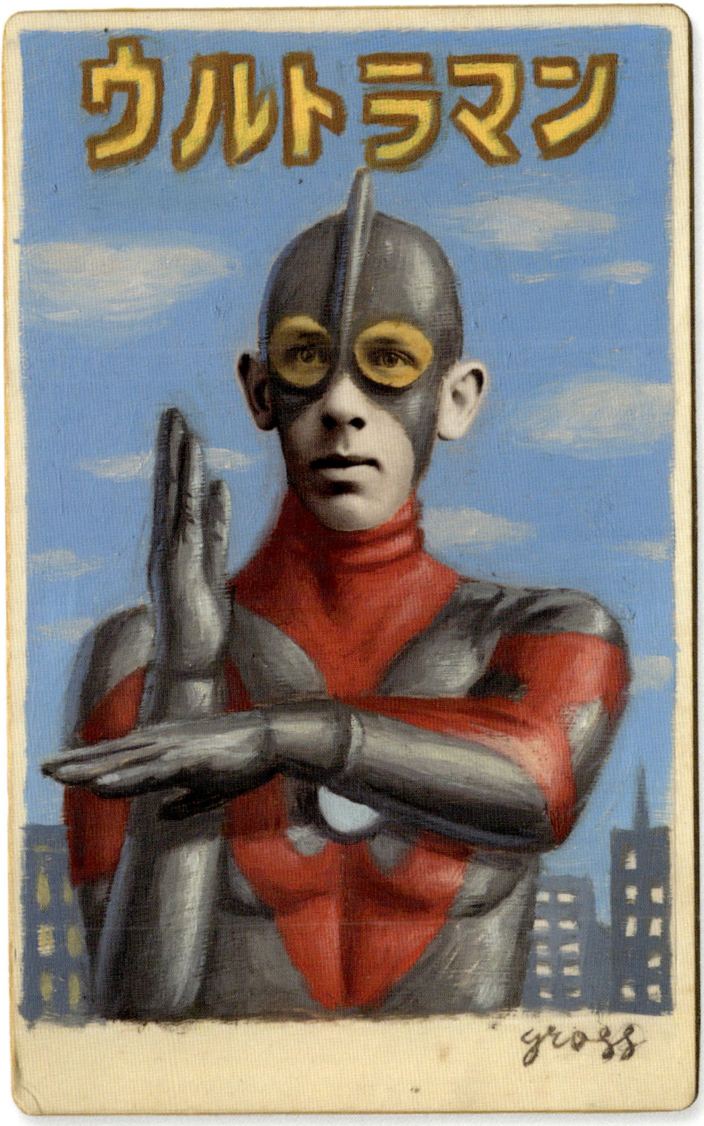
ウルトラマン
gross

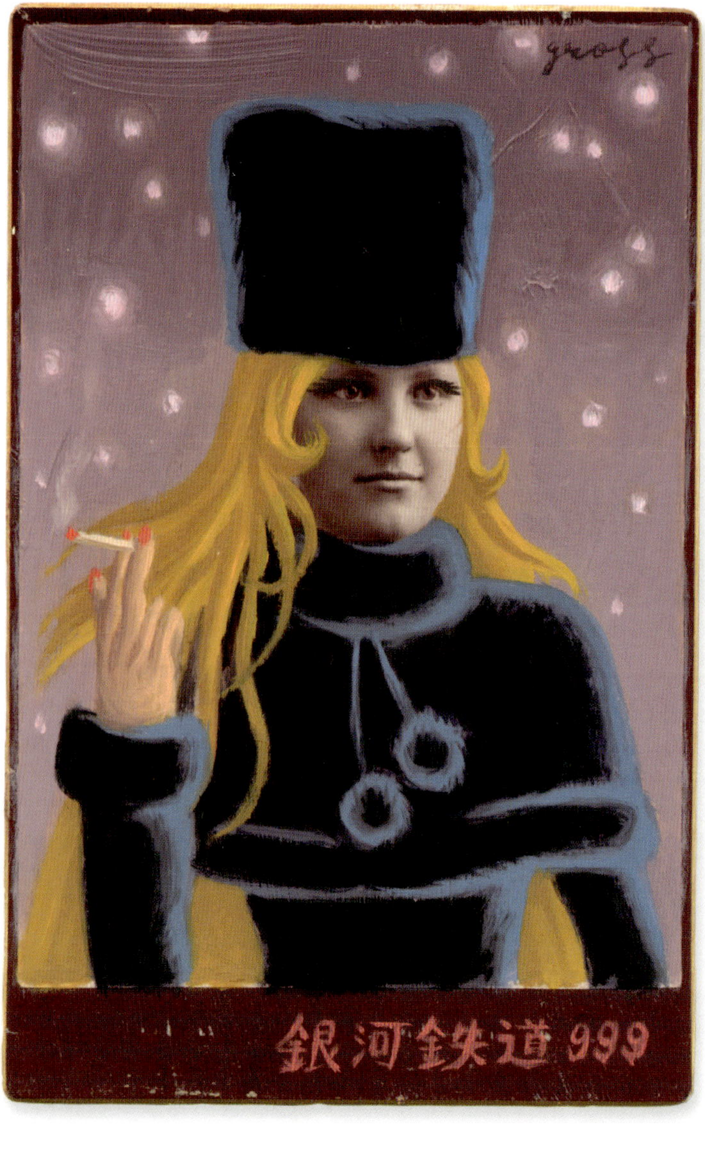
grogg
銀河鉄道999

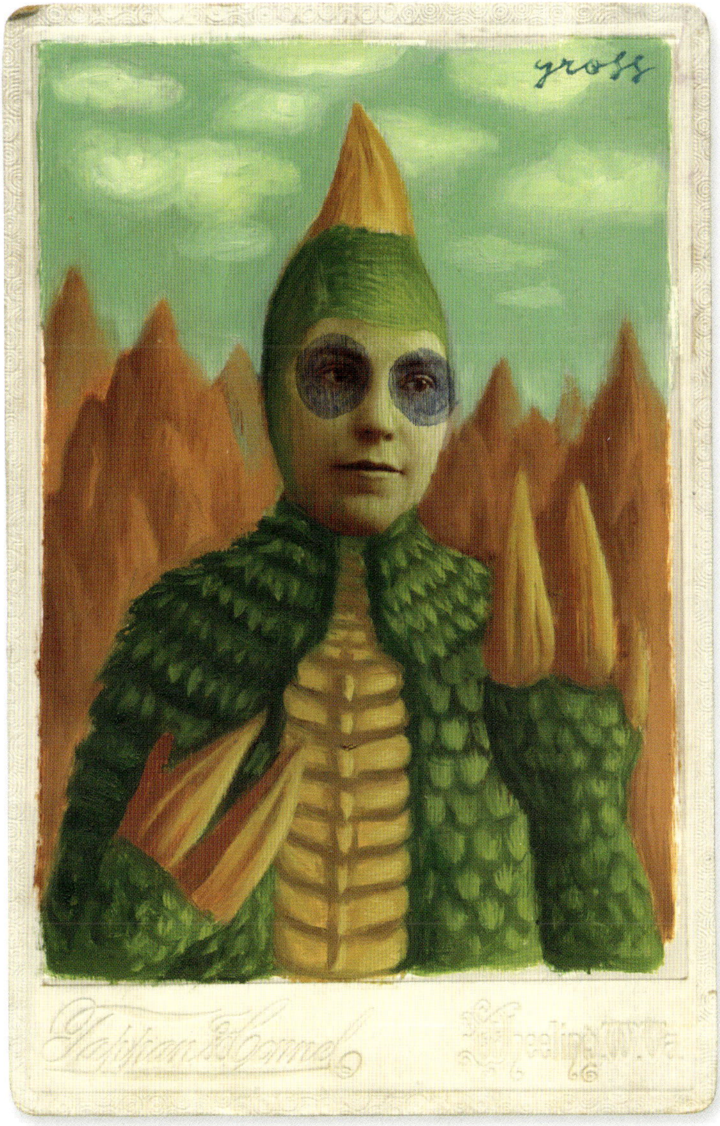
gross

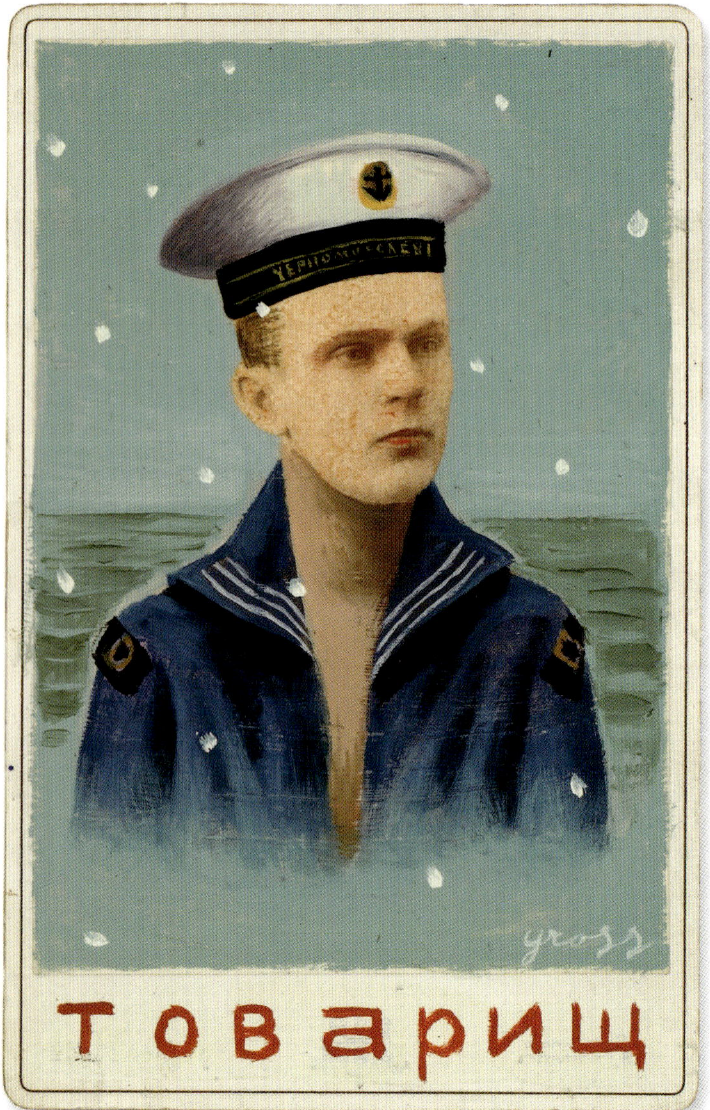
товарищ

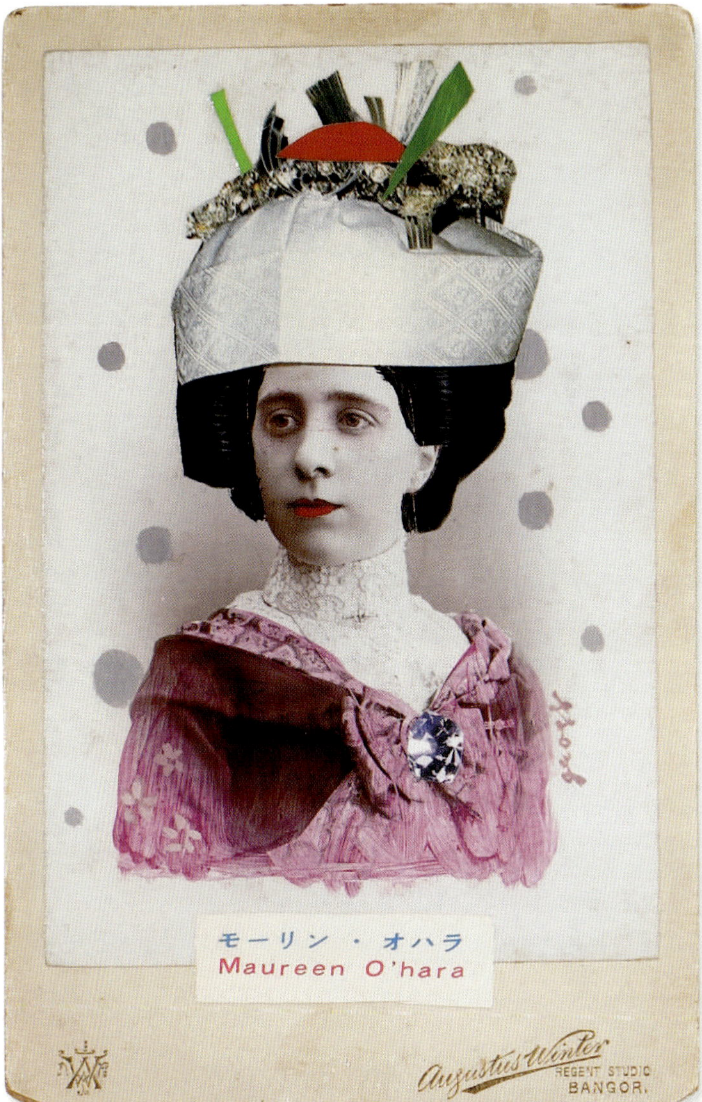
モーリン・オハラ
Maureen O'hara
Augustus Winter
REGENT STUDIO
BANGOR.

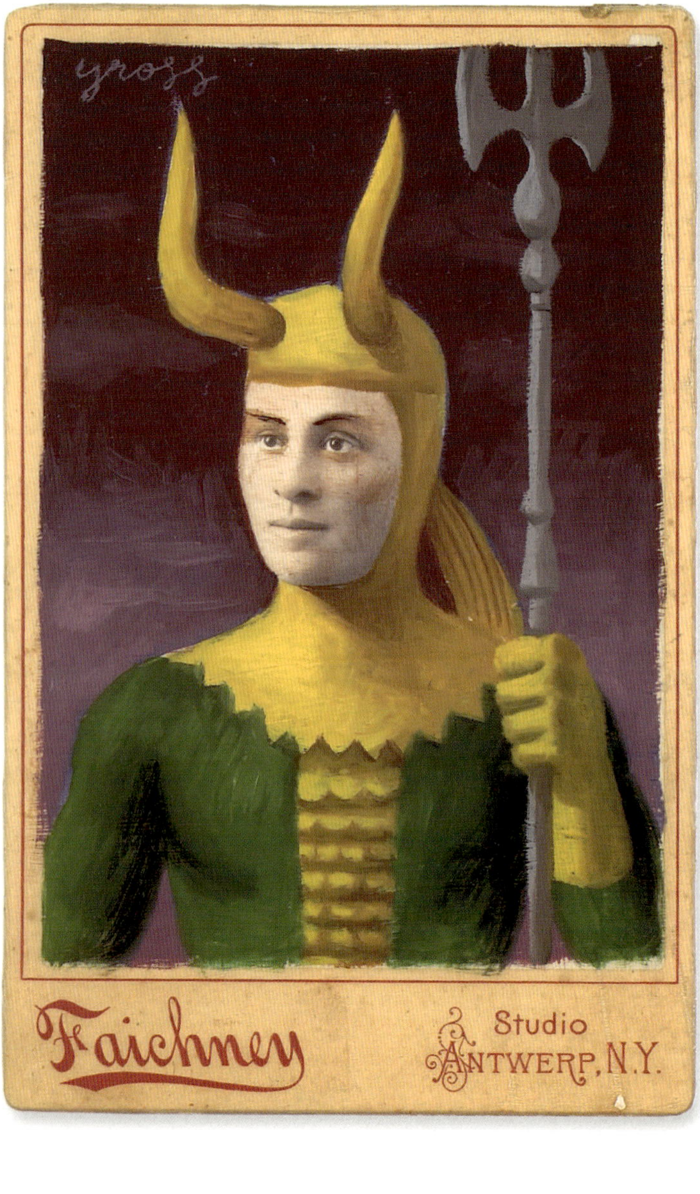
gross
Faichney
Studio
Antwerp, N.Y.

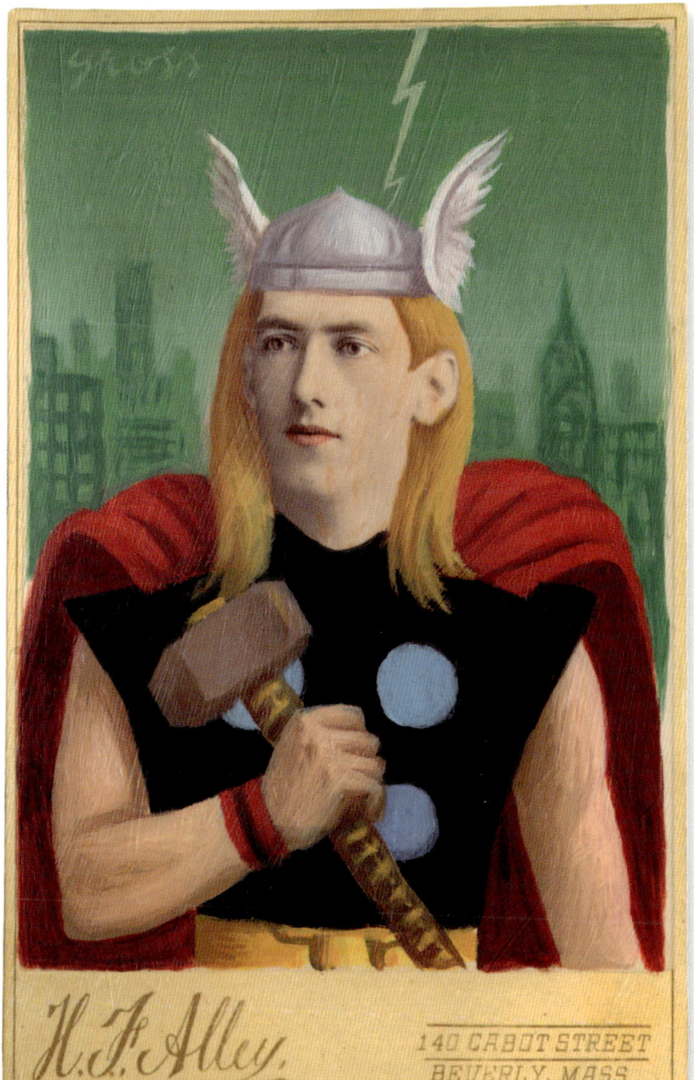
H. F. Alley.
140 CABOT STREET
BEVERLY, MASS.

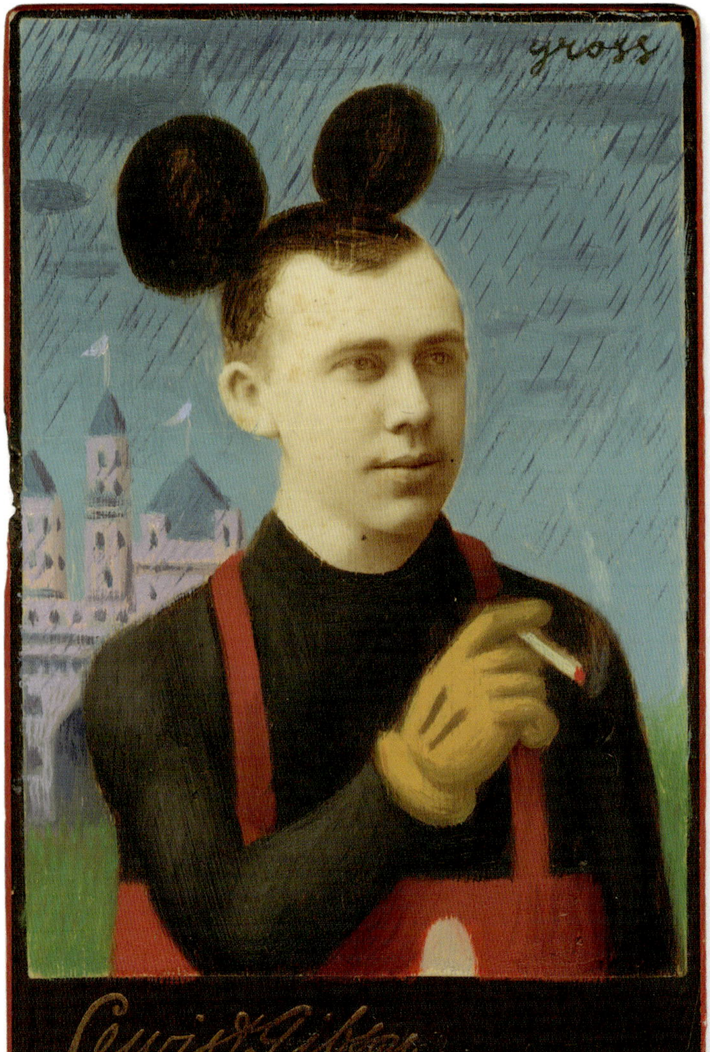
gross
Lewis & Gibbon
ANN ARBOR, MICH.

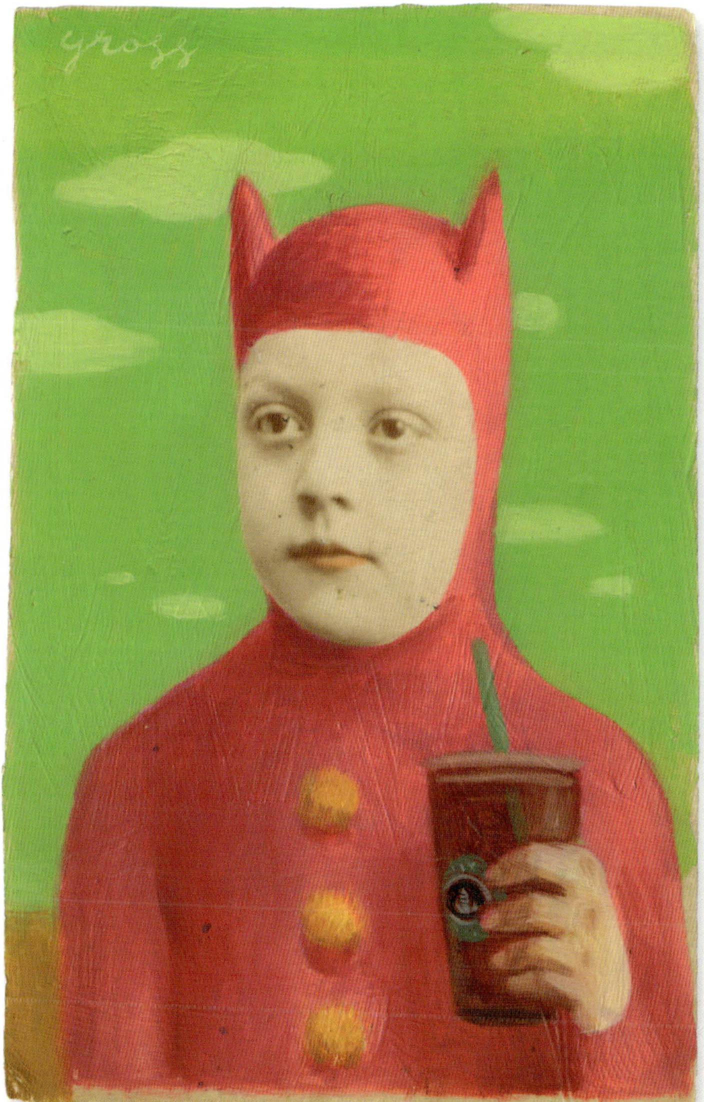
gross

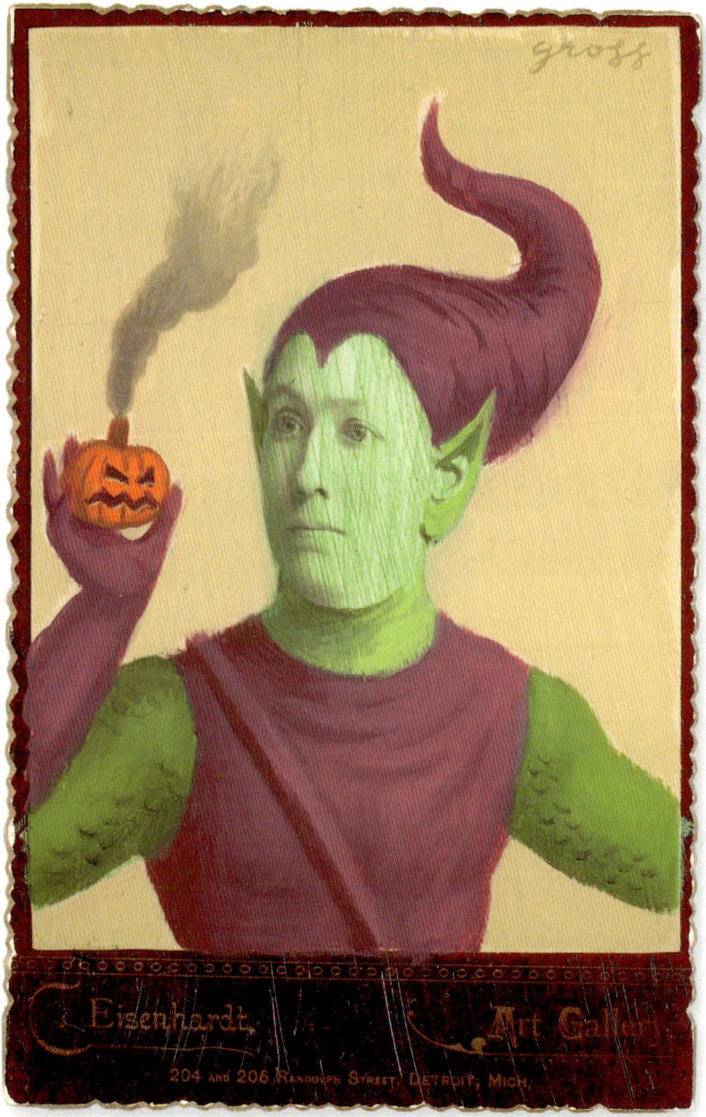
gross
Eisenhardt Art Gallery
204 and 206 Randolph Street, Detroit, Mich.

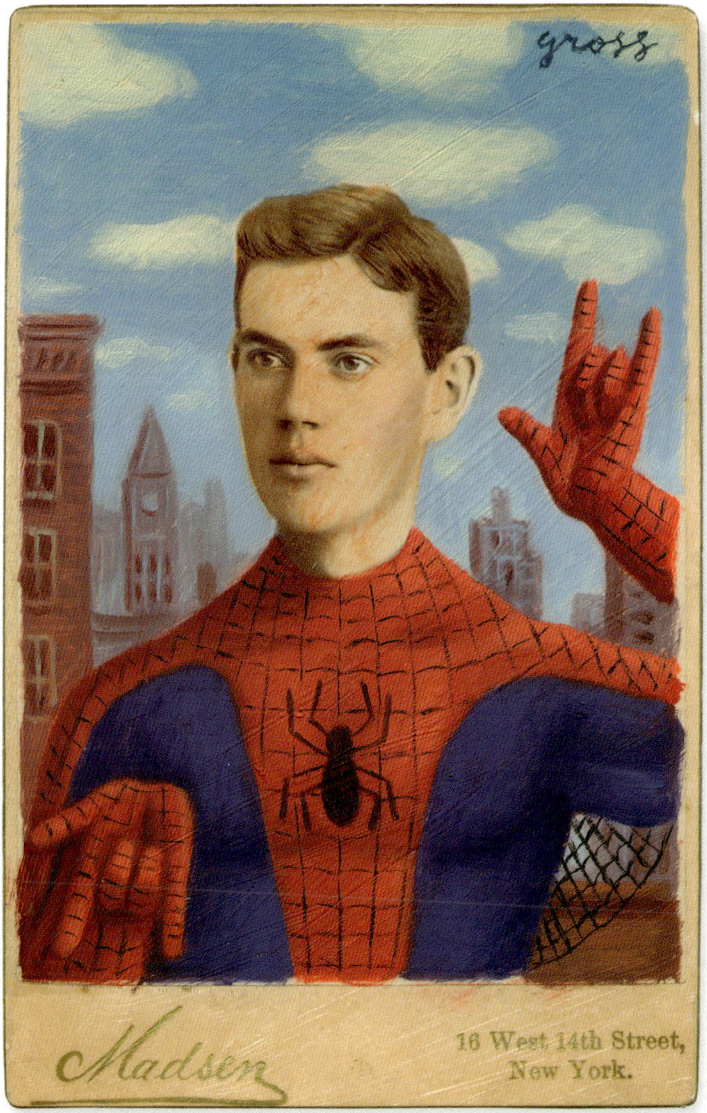
gross
Madsen
16 West 14th Street,
New York.

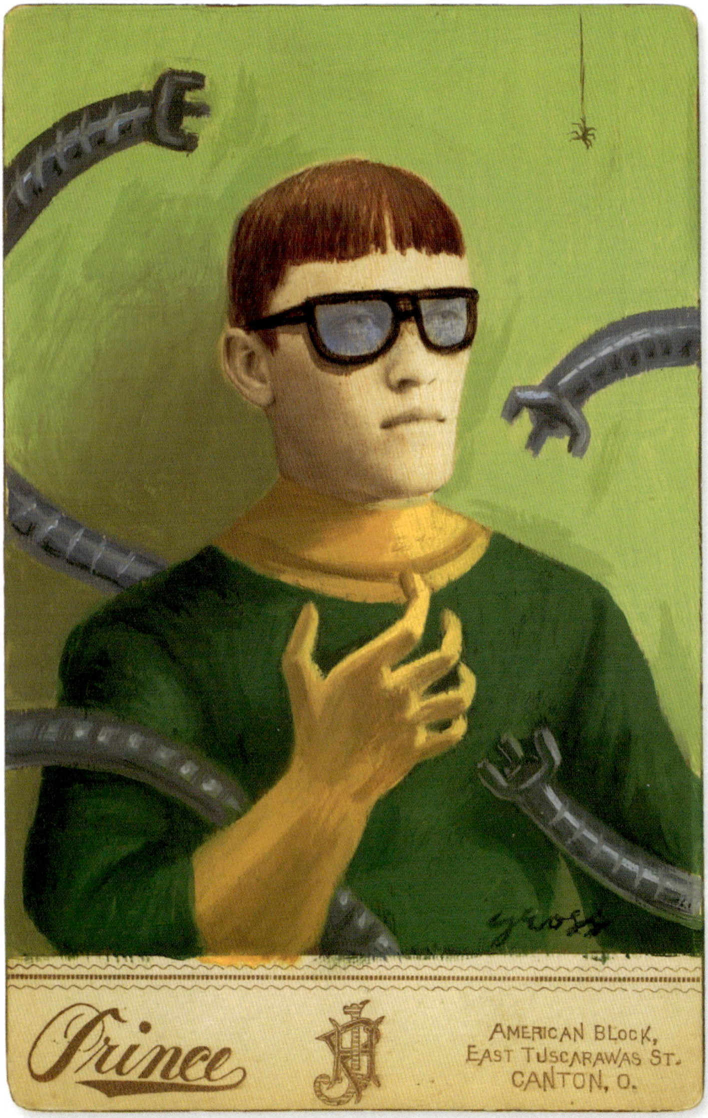
Prince
AMERICAN BLOCK,
EAST TUSCARAWAS ST.
CANTON, O.

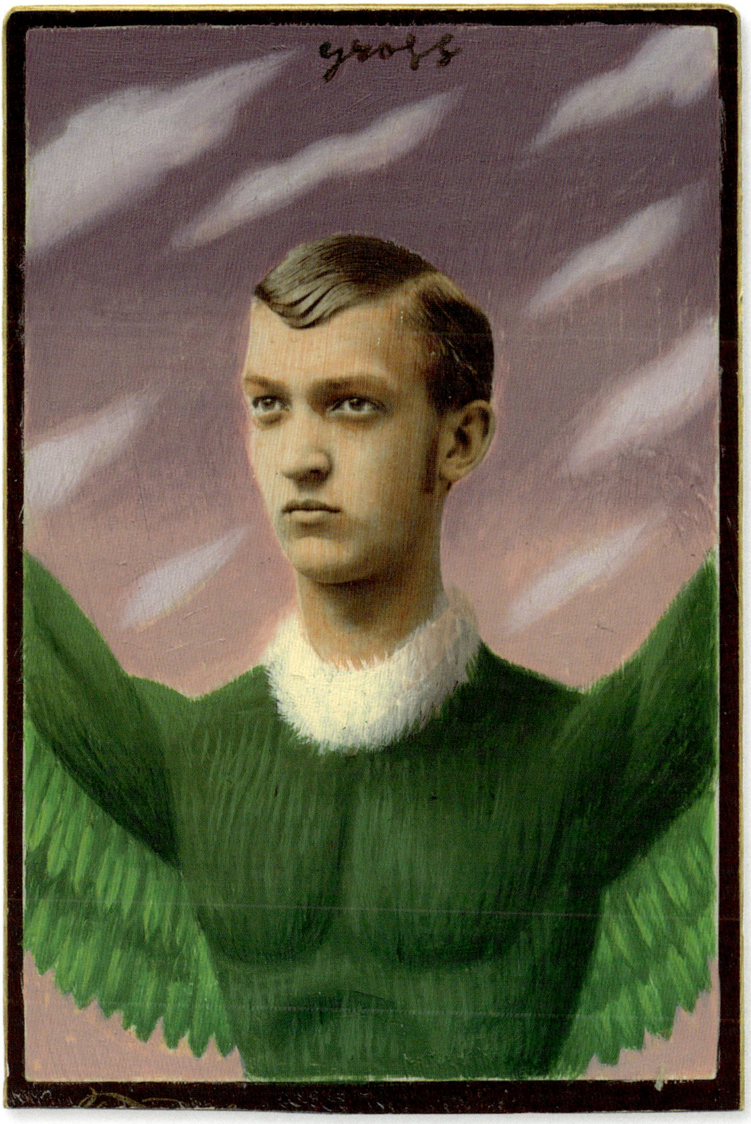

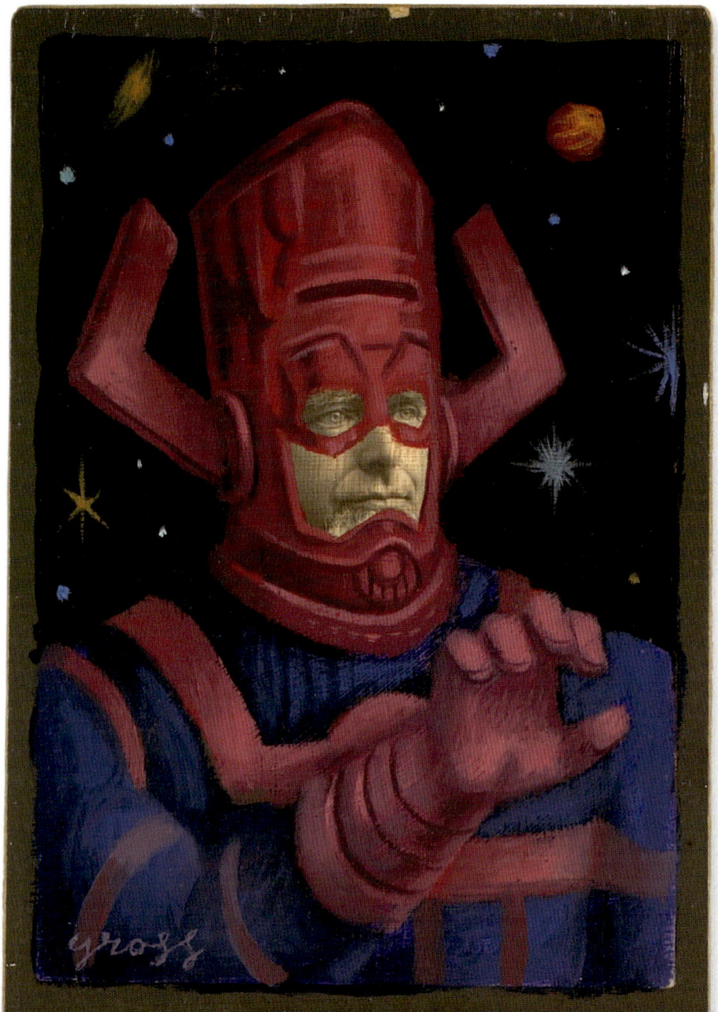

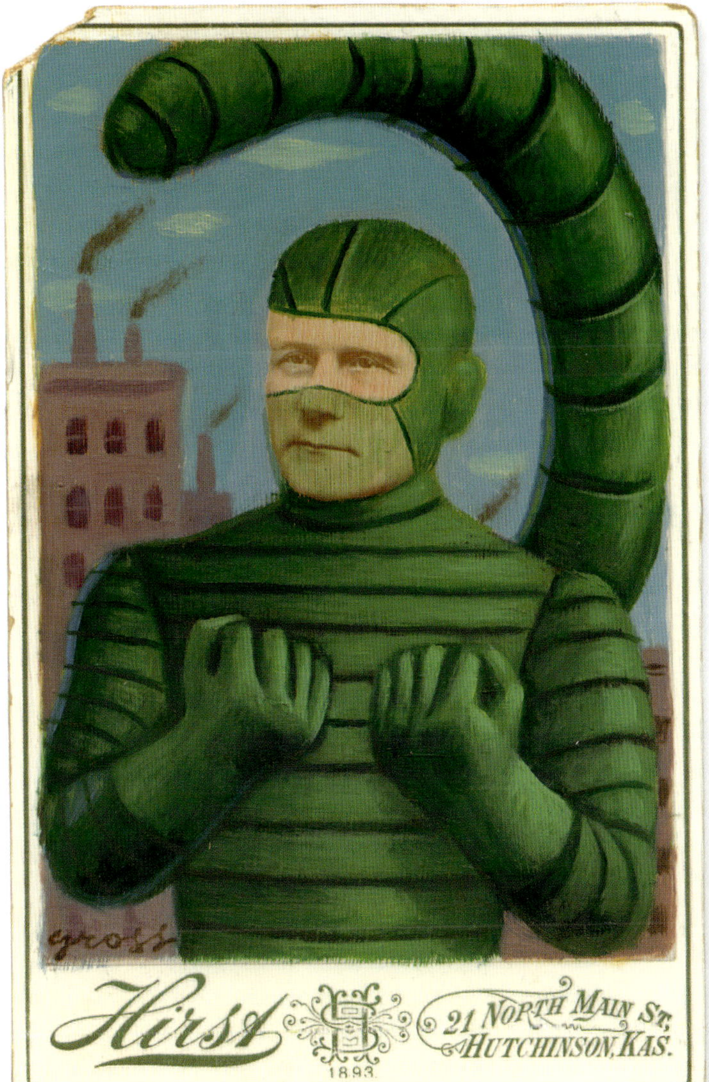
gross
Hirst
21 NORTH MAIN ST,
HUTCHINSON, KAS.
1893

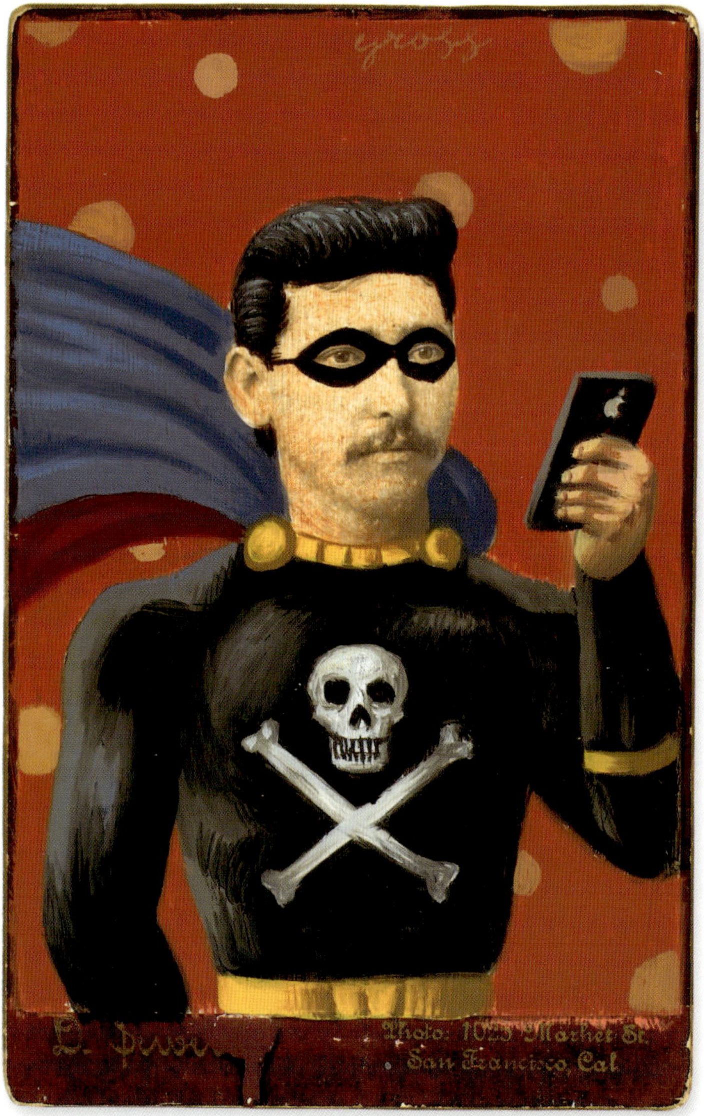
San Francisco, Cal

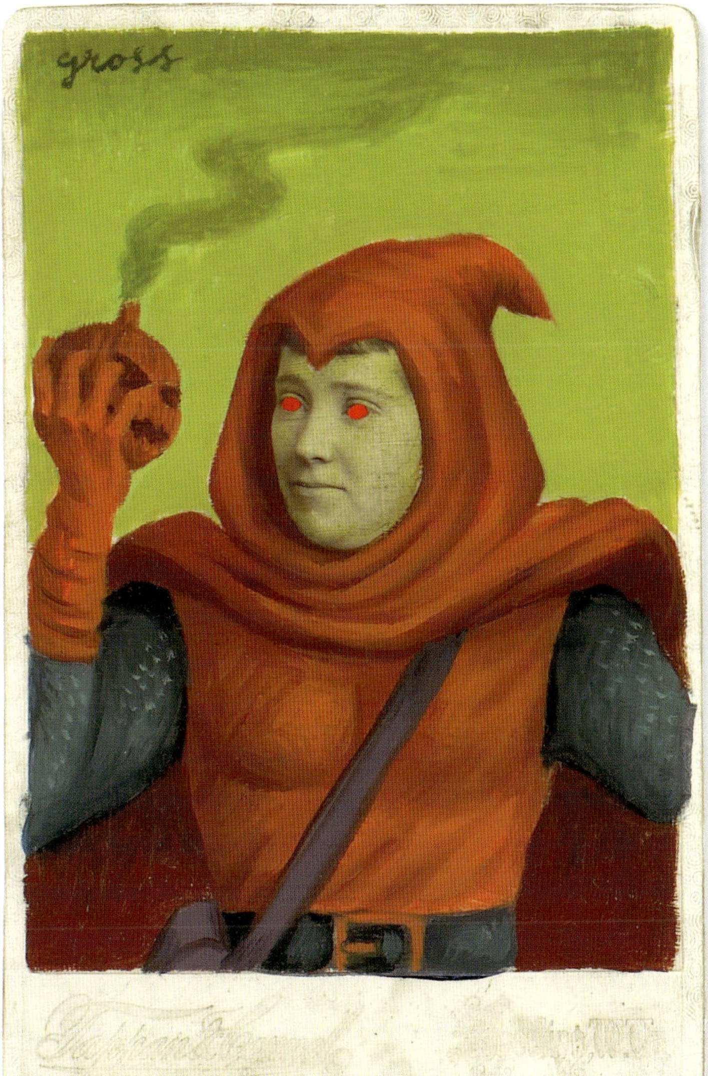
gross

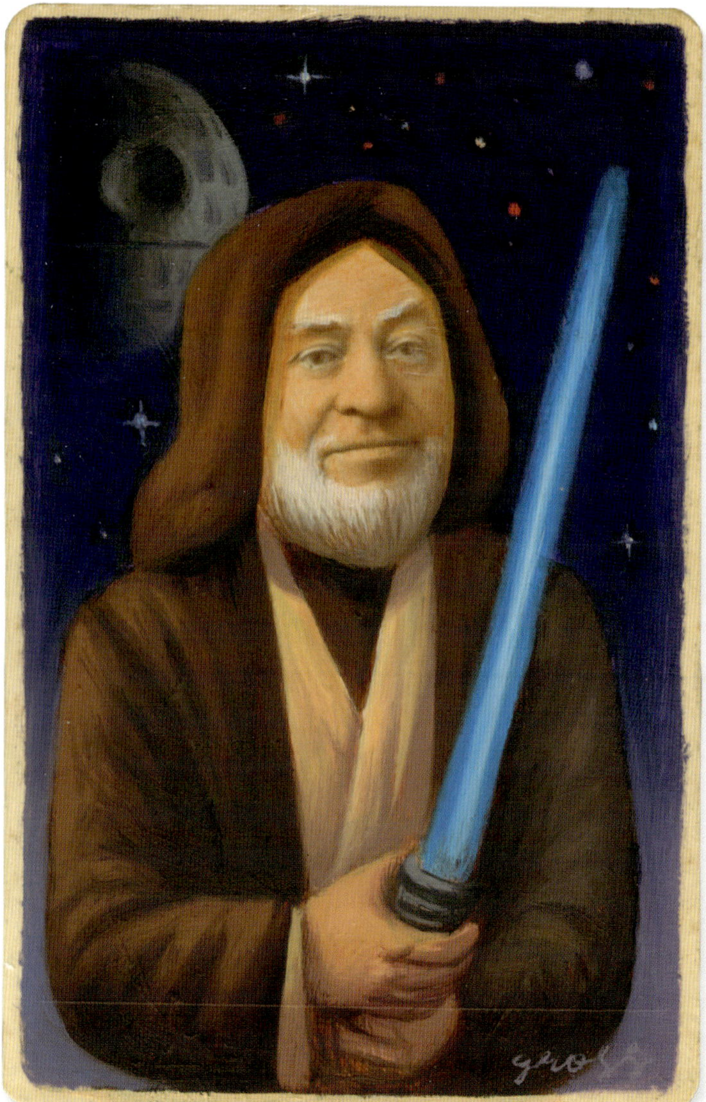

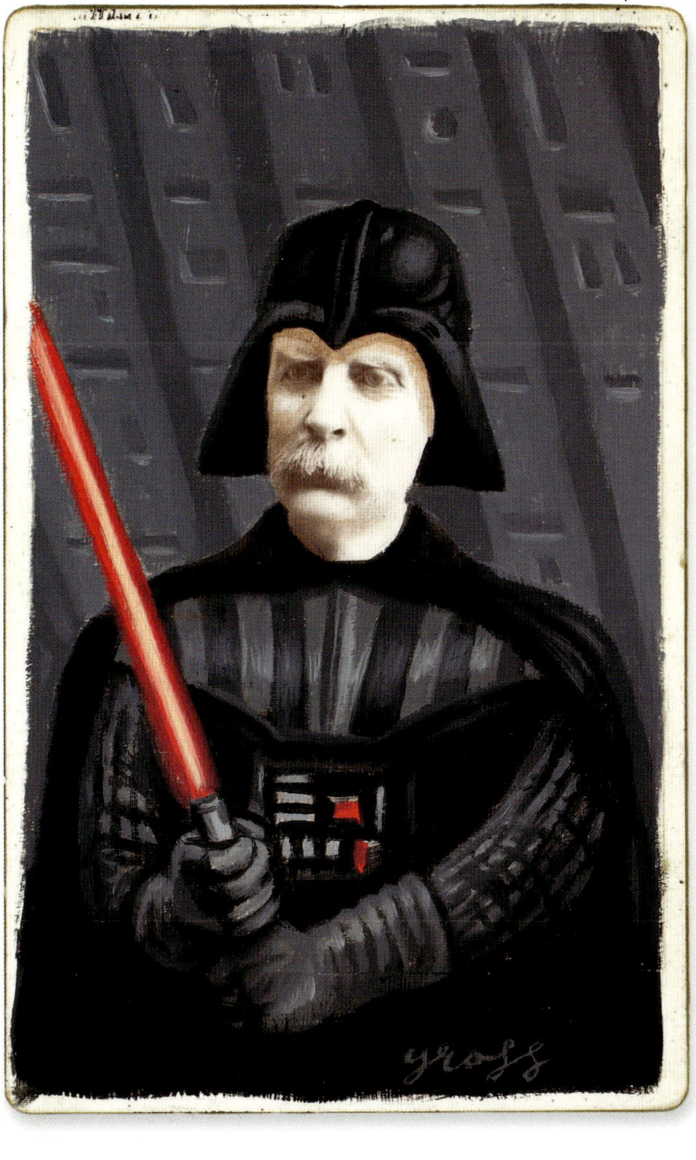
gross

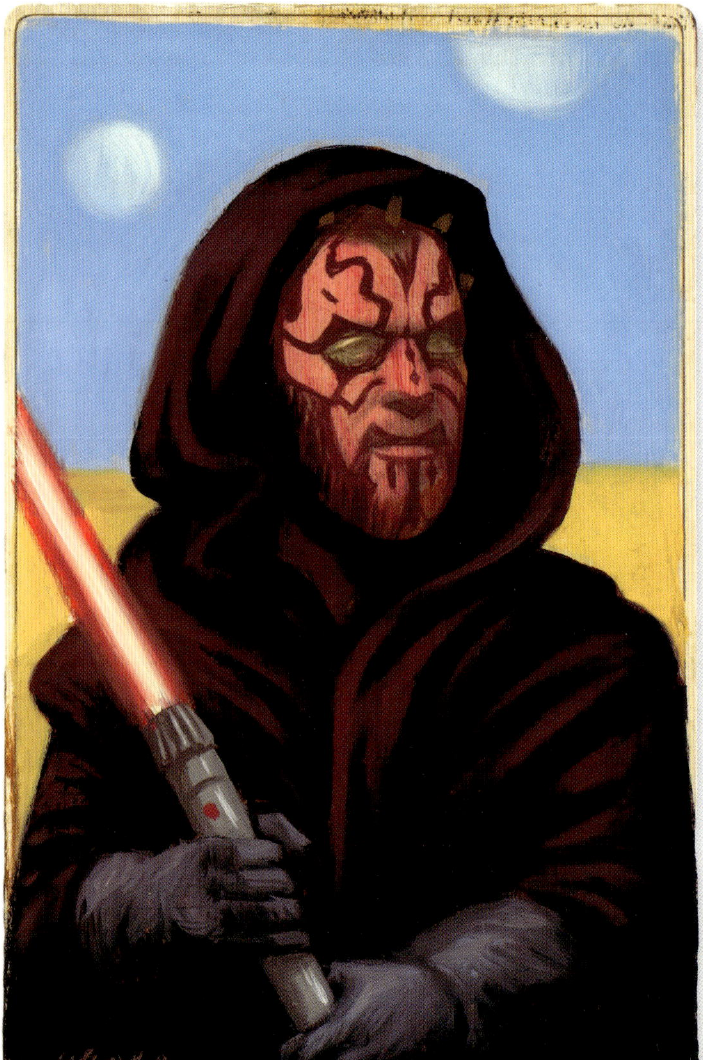

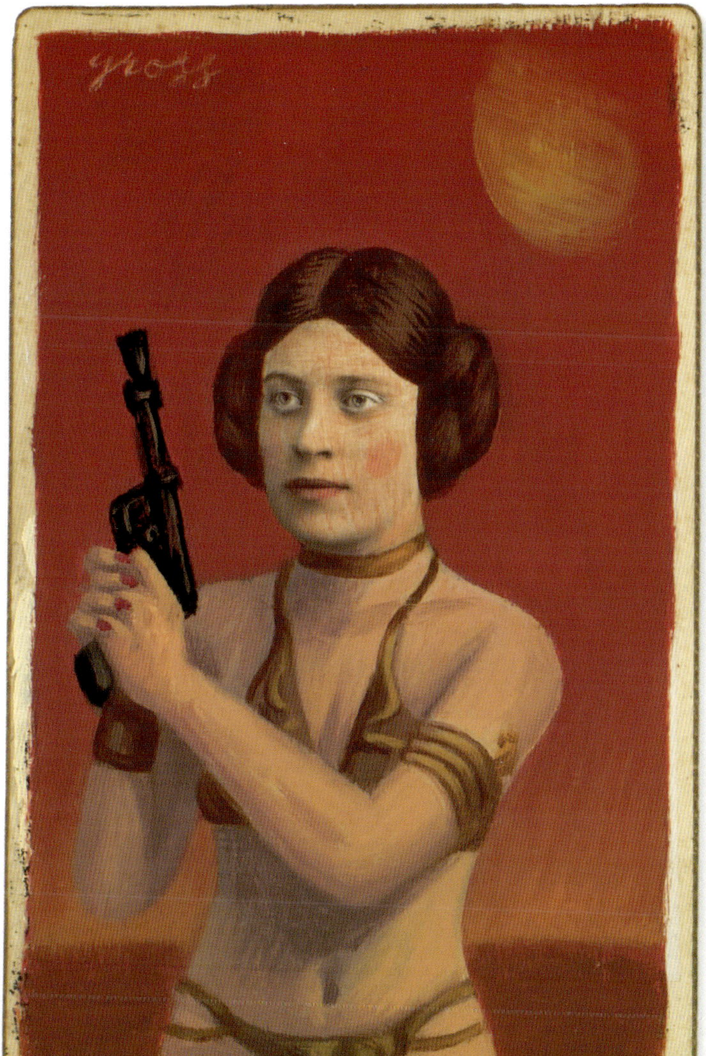

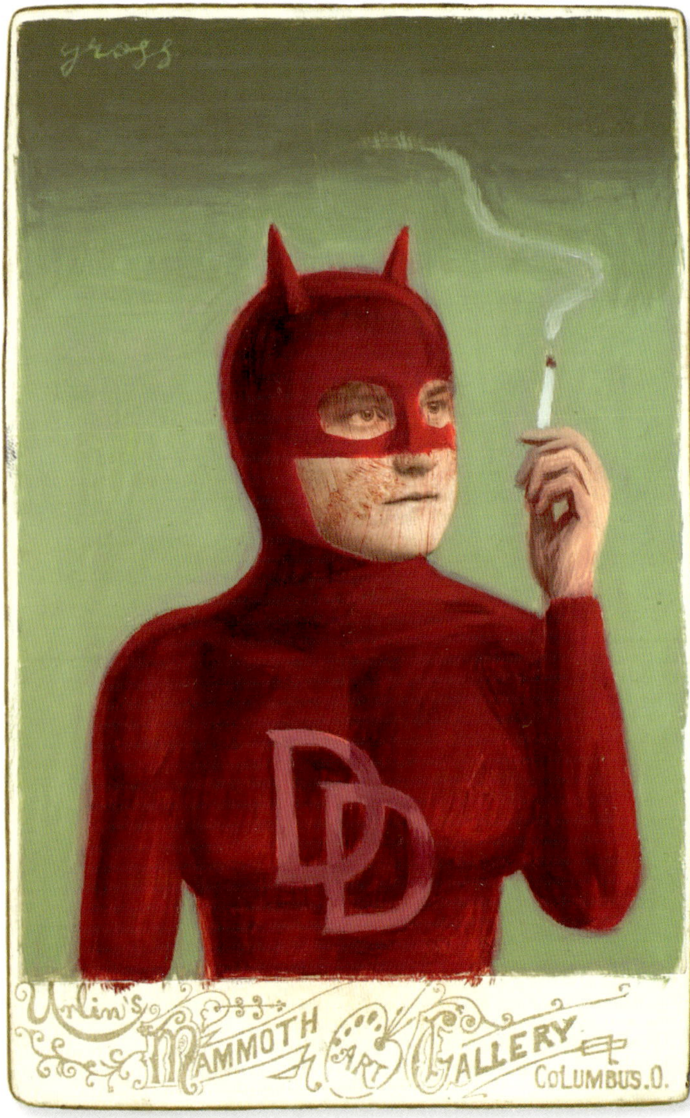
Urlin's
MAMMOTH
ART
GALLERY
COLUMBUS.O.

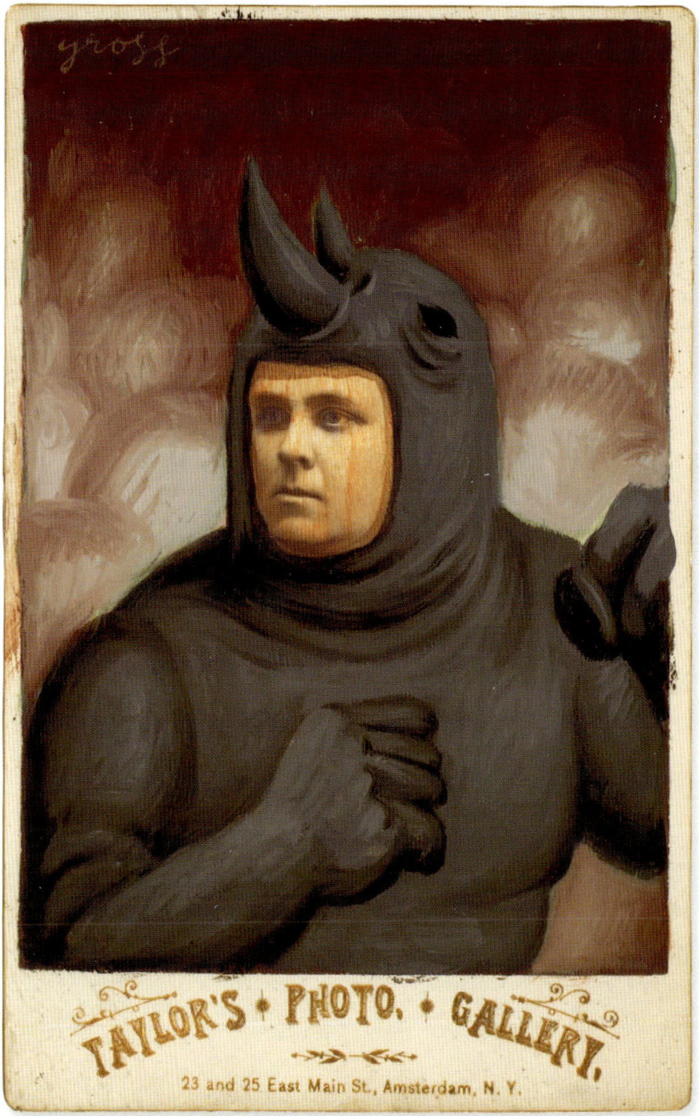
gross
TAYLOR'S PHOTO. GALLERY.
23 and 25 East Main St., Amsterdam, N. Y.

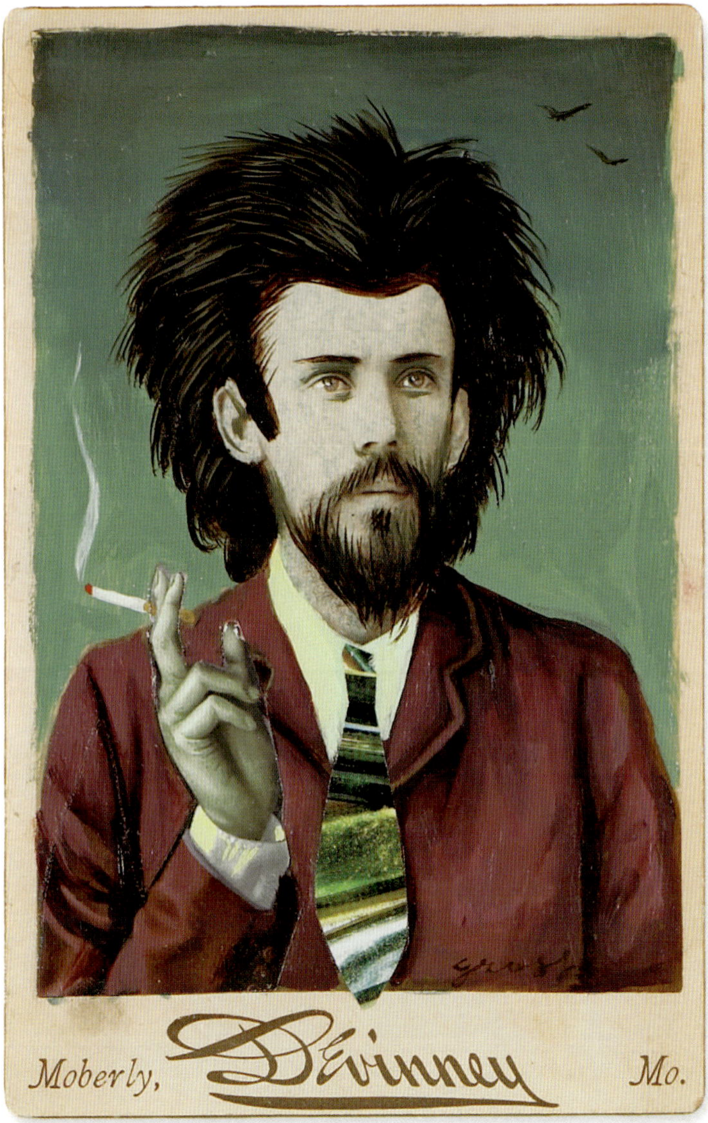
Moberly,
Swinney
Mo.

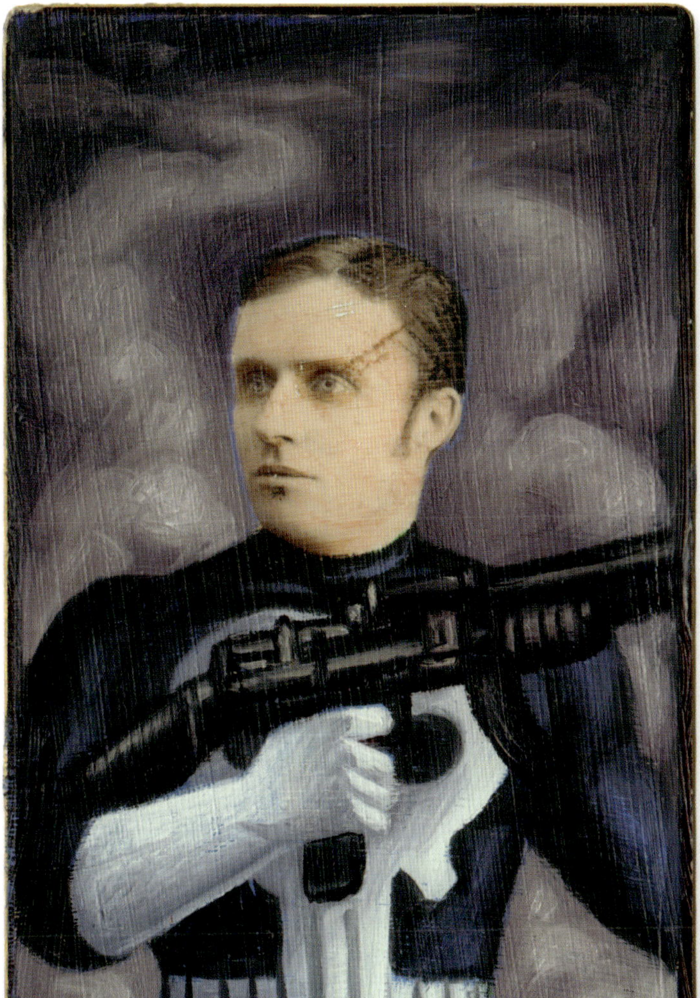
gross

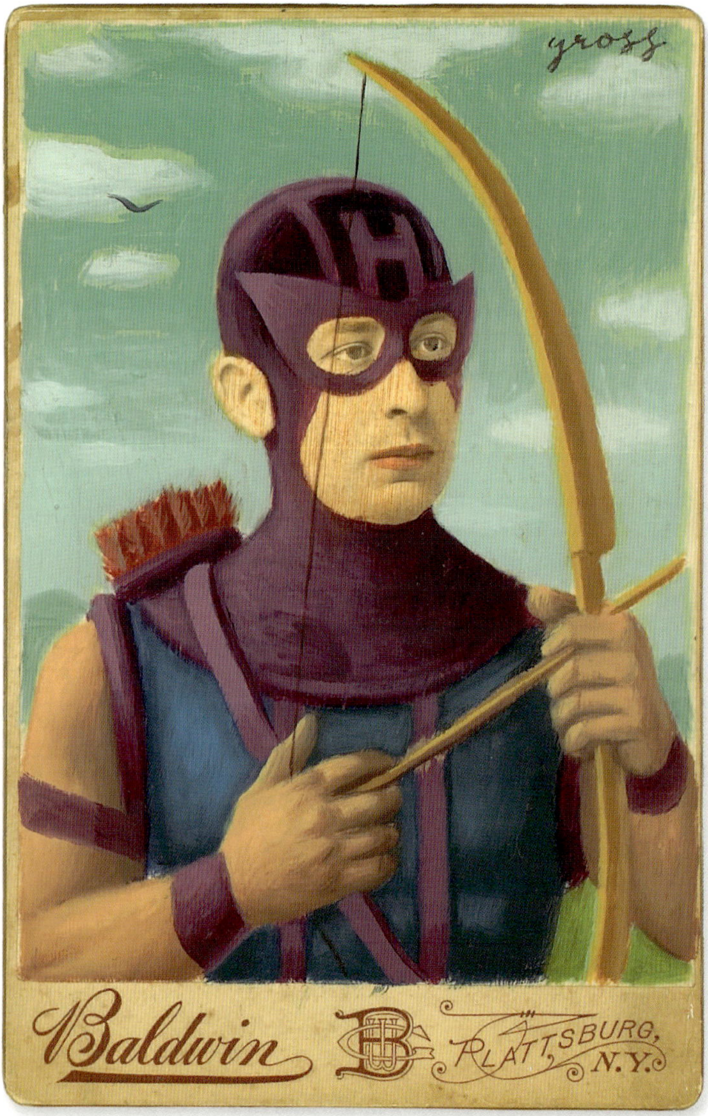
gross
Baldwin
PLATTSBURG,
N.Y.

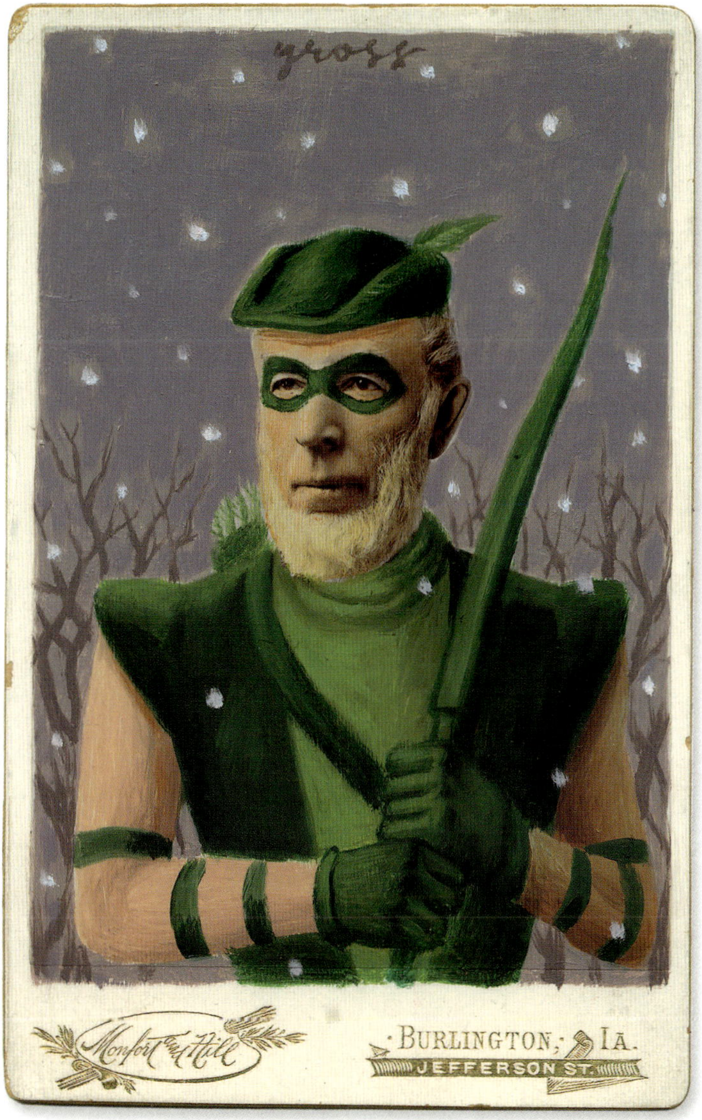
gross
Monfort & Hill
BURLINGTON, IA.
JEFFERSON ST.

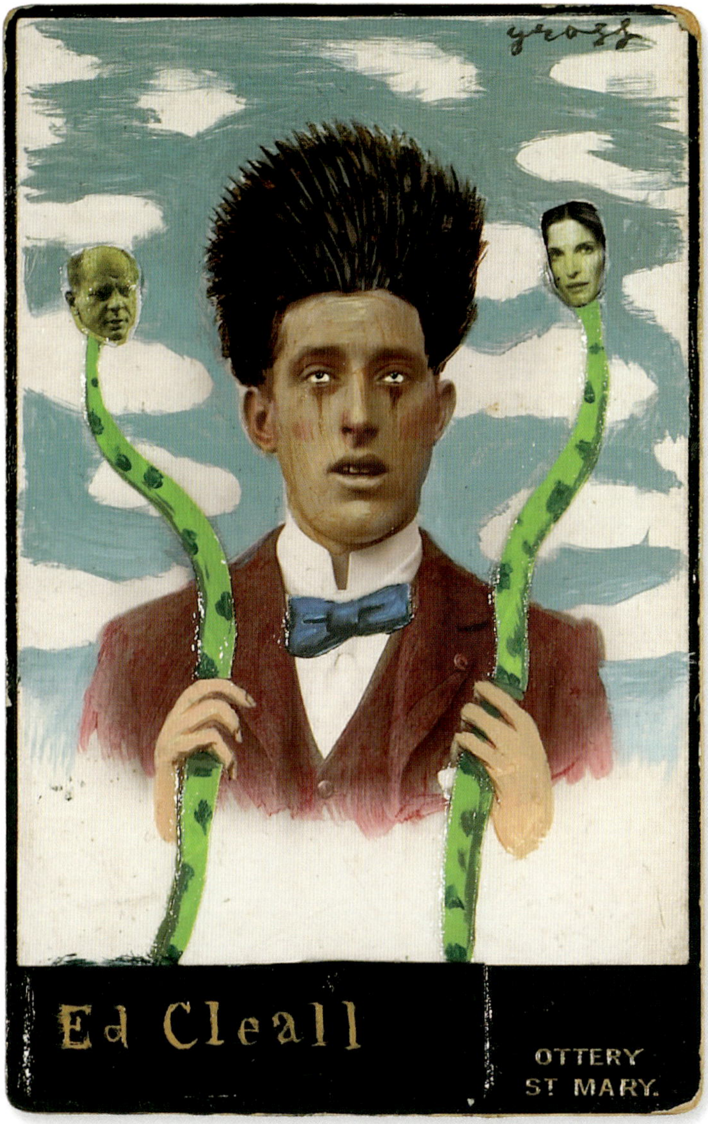

yrozz
Ed Cleall
OTTERY
ST MARY.

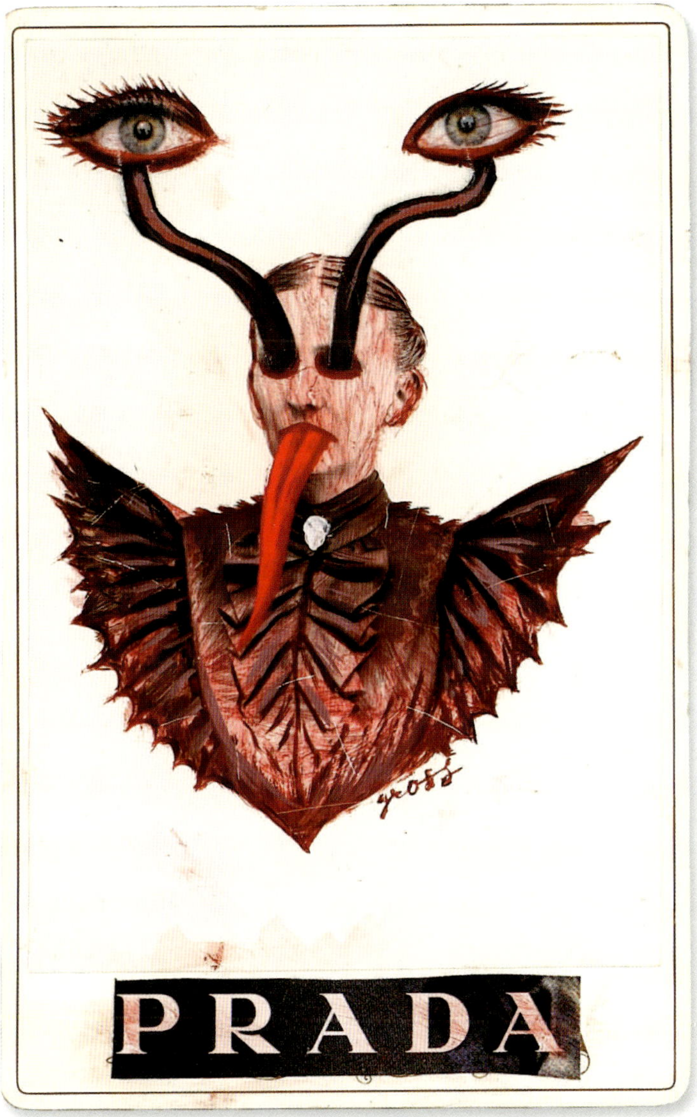
PRADA

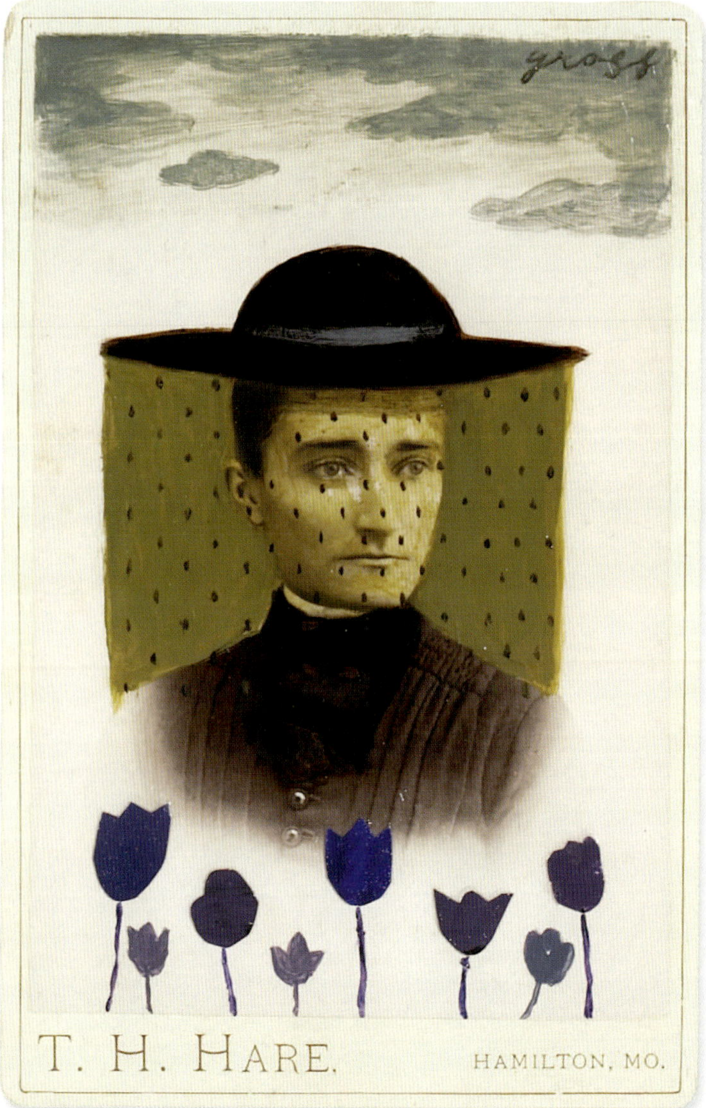
grogg
T. H. HARE.
HAMILTON, MO.

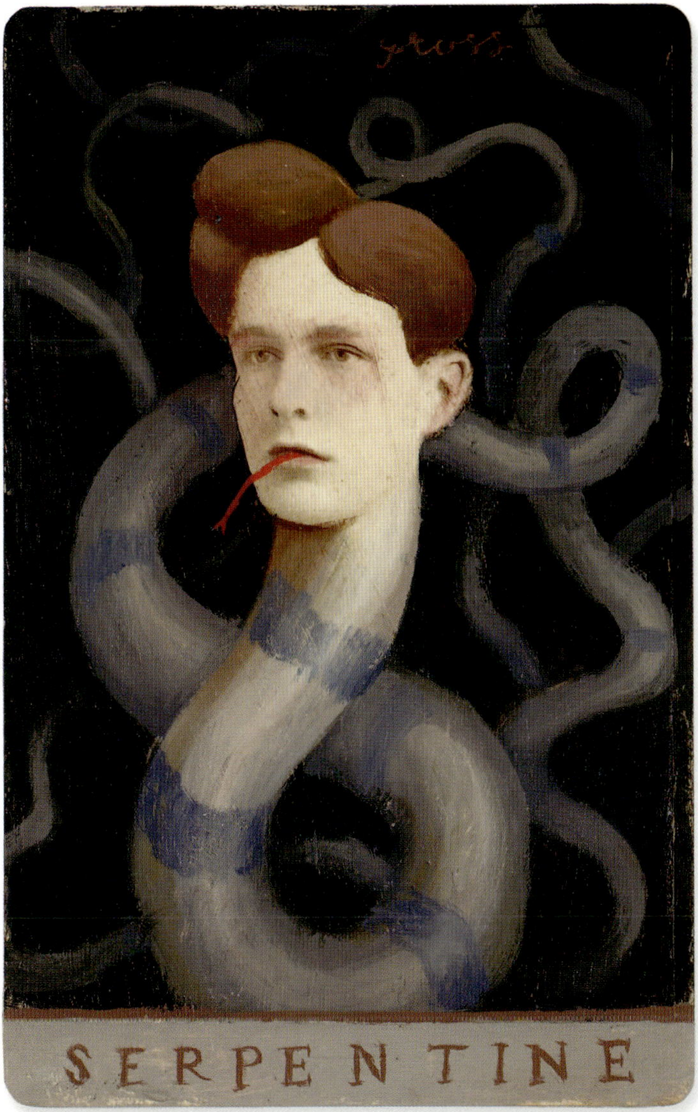
SERPENTINE

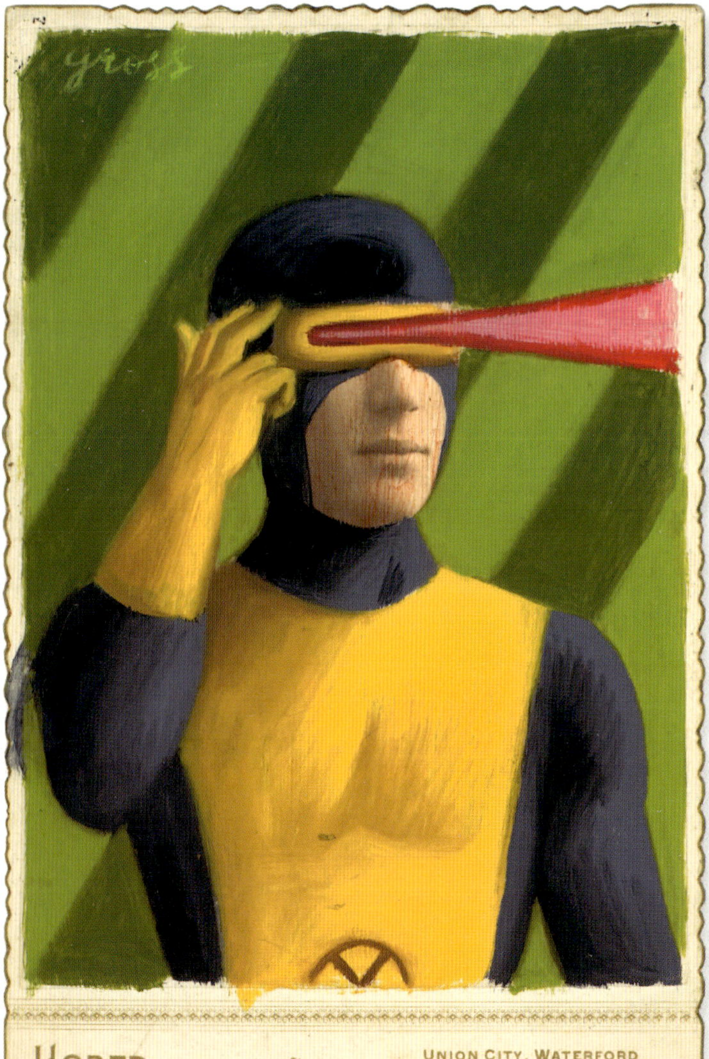
Hearn,
UNION CITY, WATERFORD
AND SPARTANSBURG, PA.

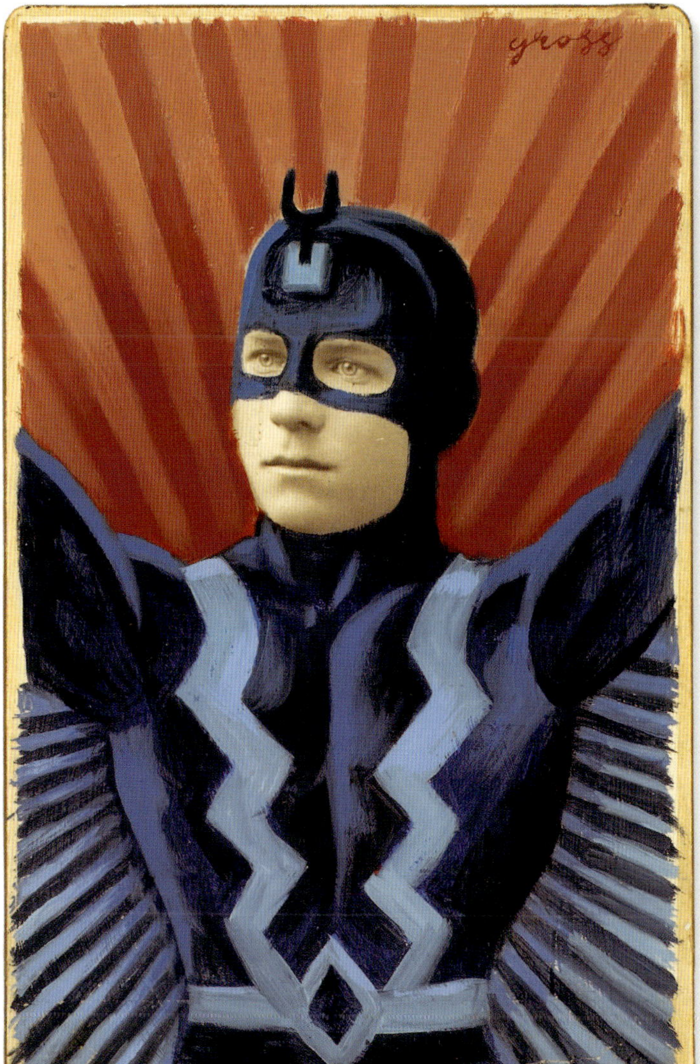
gross

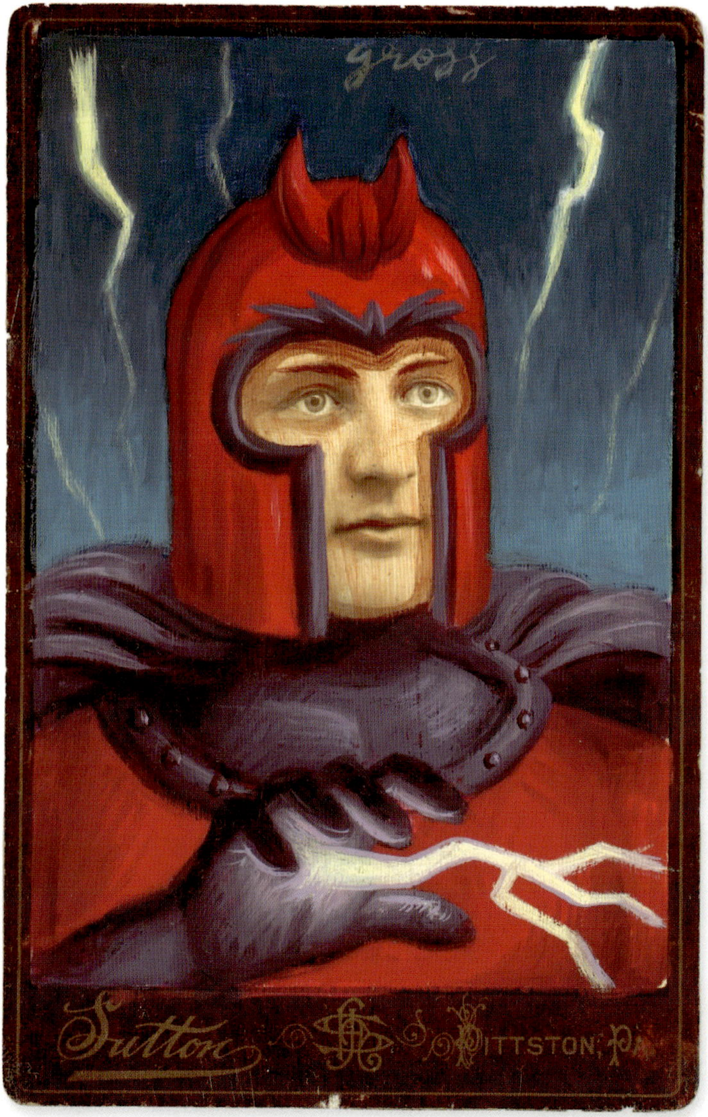
gross
Sutton
PITTSTON, PA

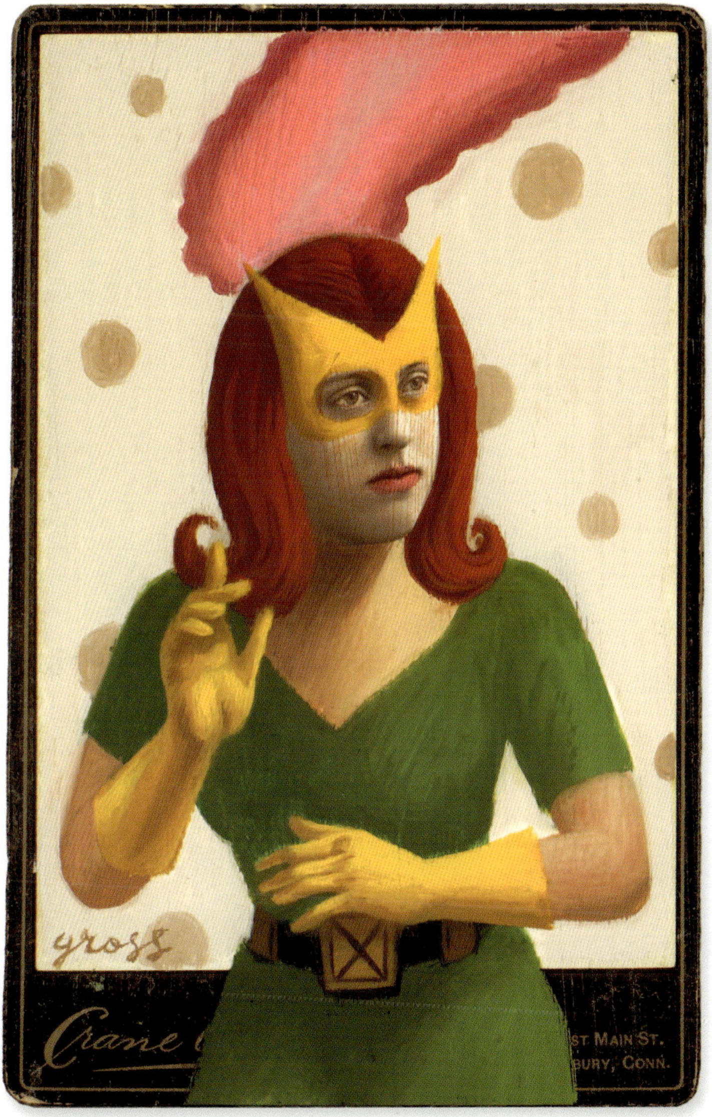
gross
Crane
ST MAIN ST.
BURY, CONN.

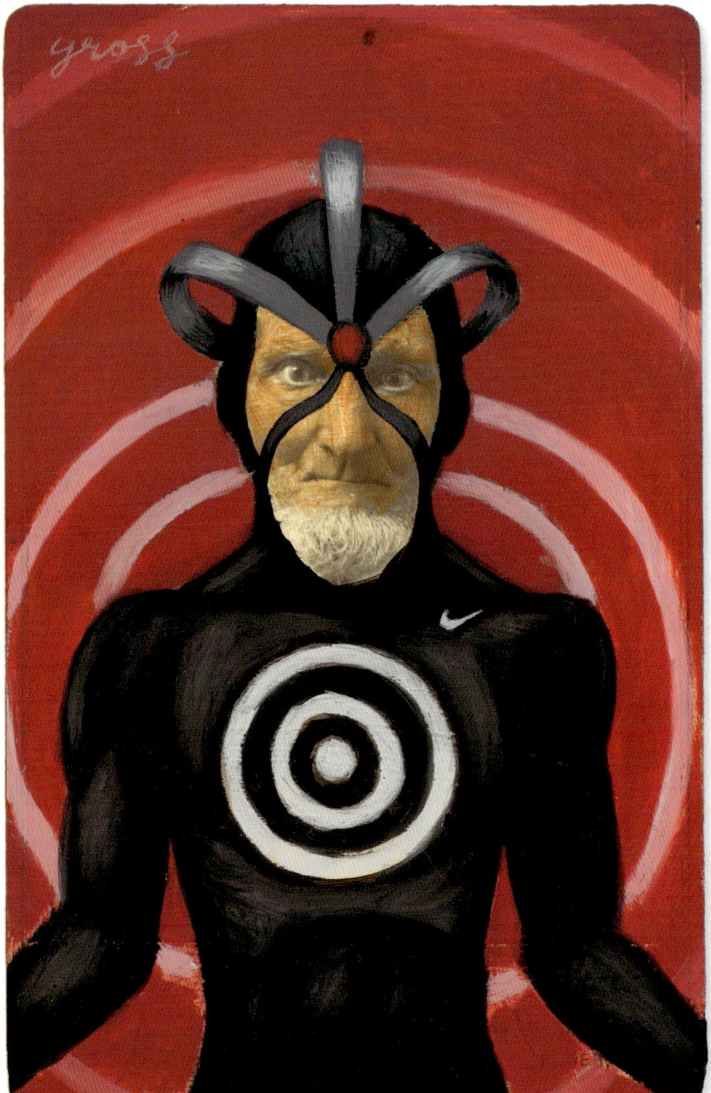
gross

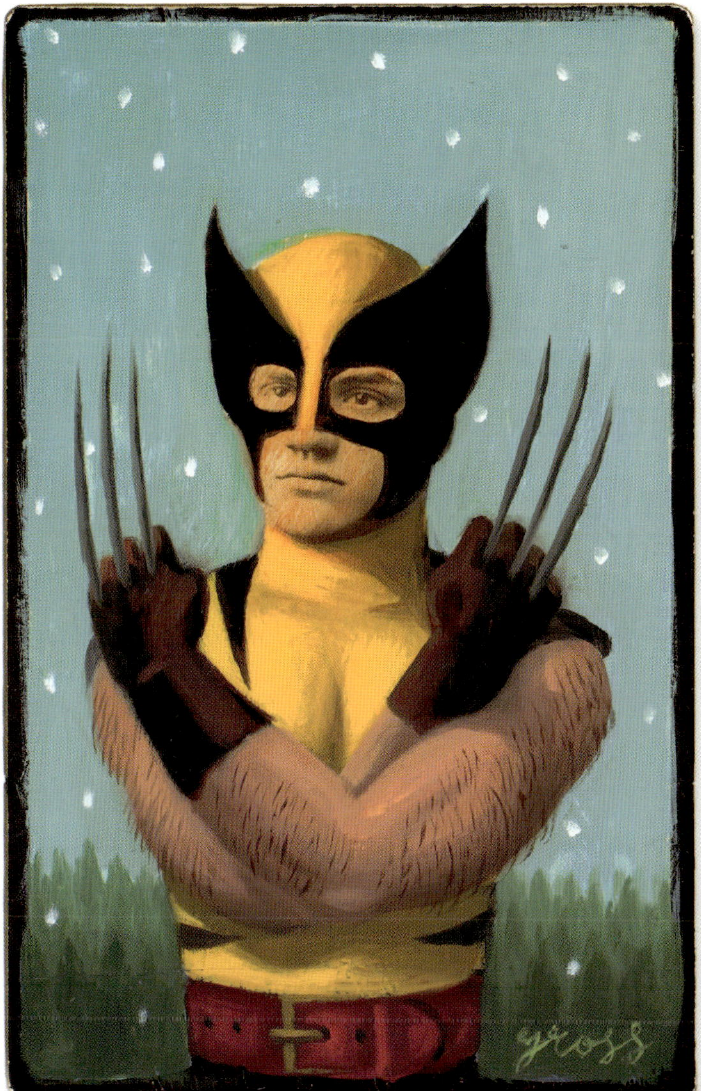
gross

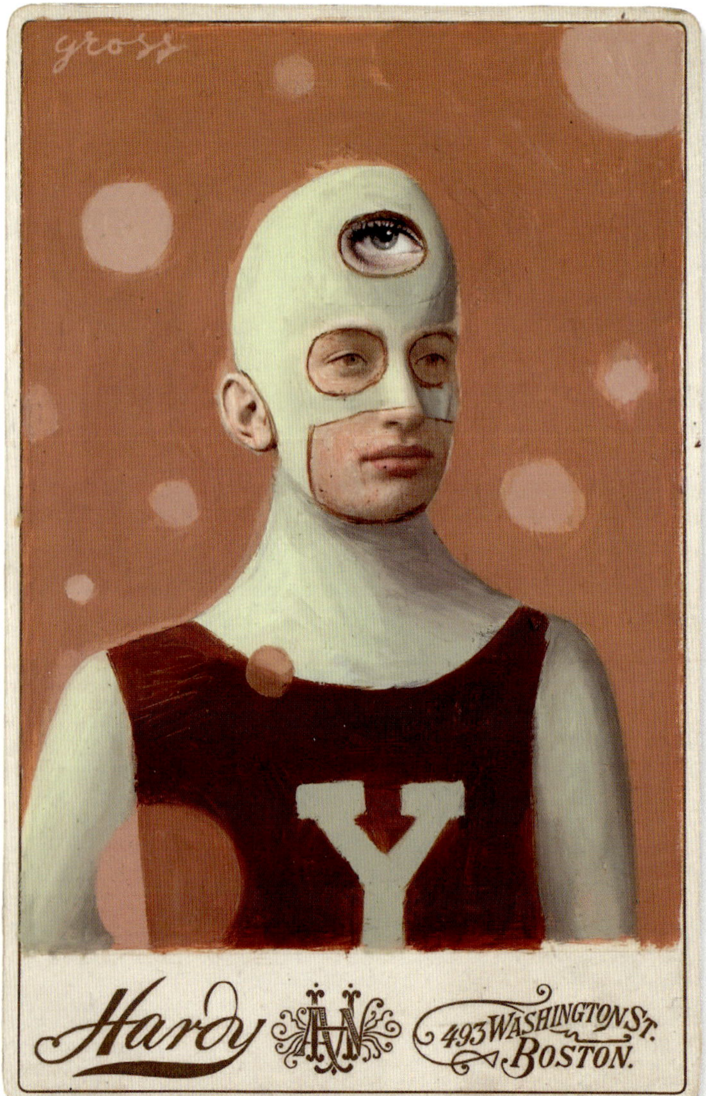
gross
Hardy
493 WASHINGTON ST.
BOSTON.

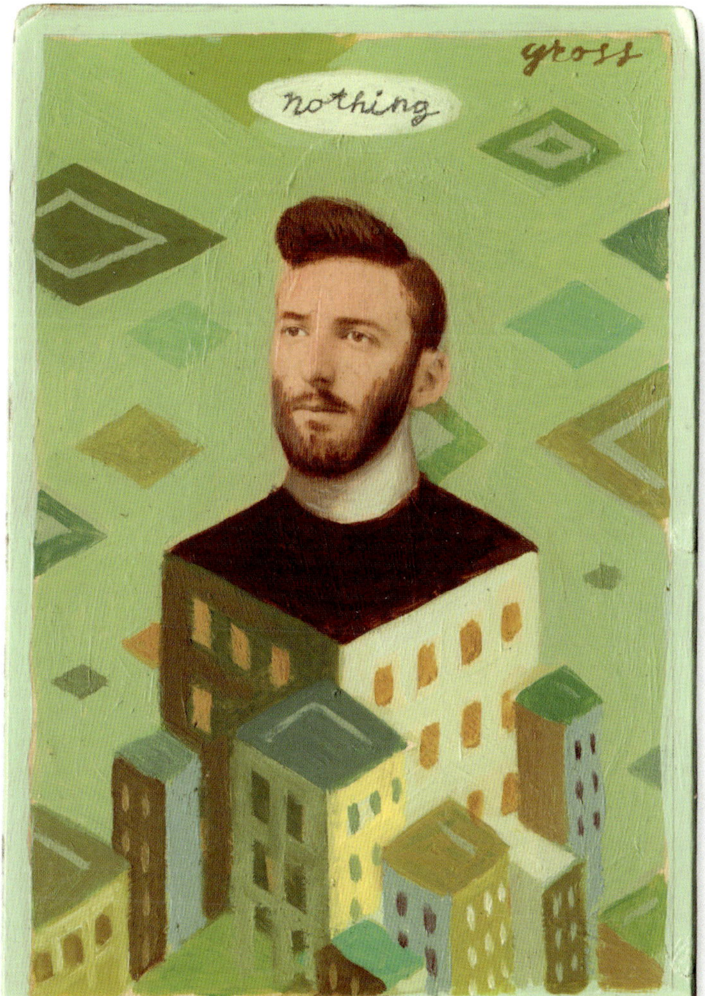
gross
nothing

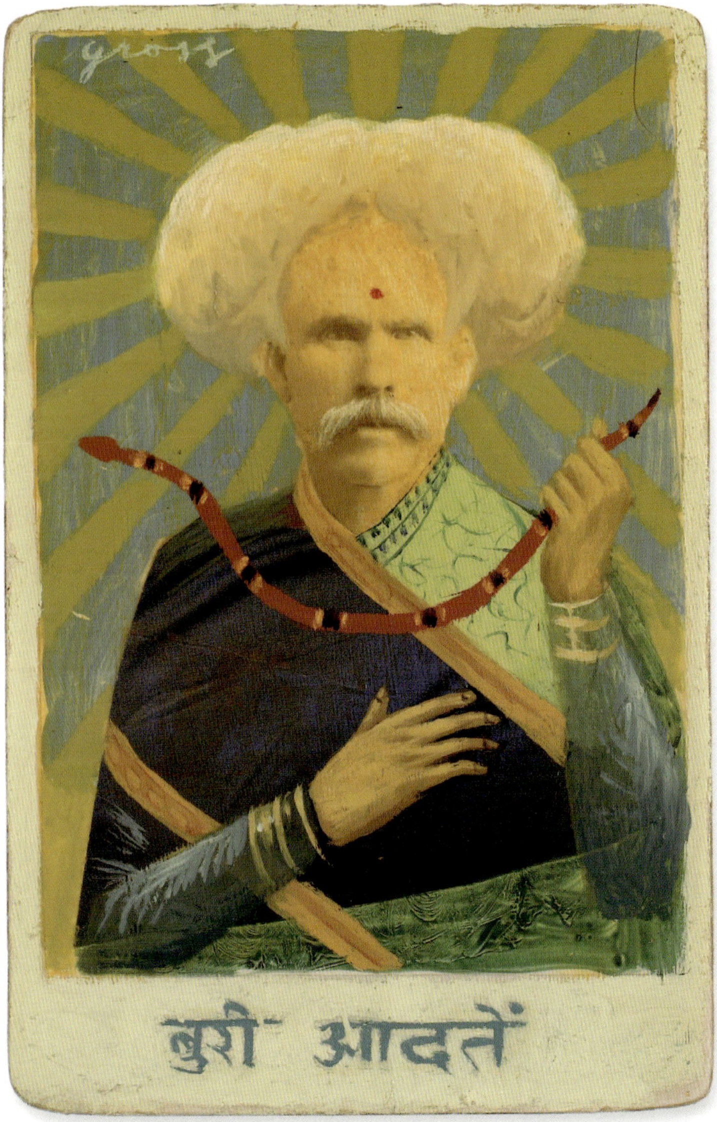
gross
बुरी आदतें

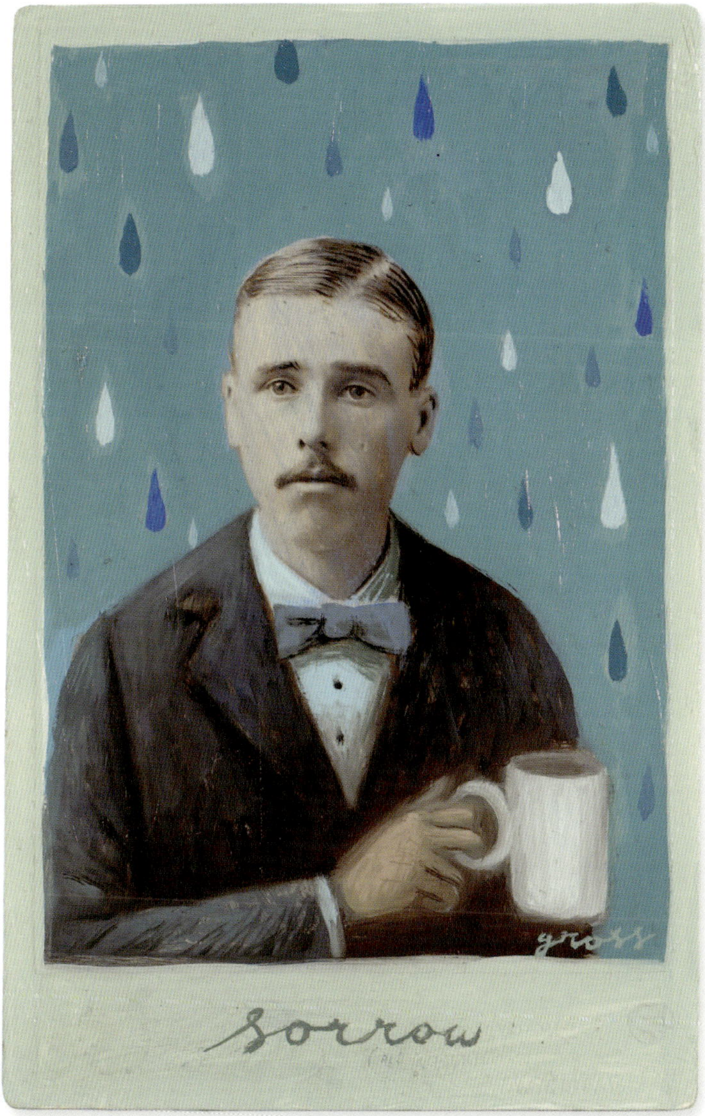
gross
Sorrow

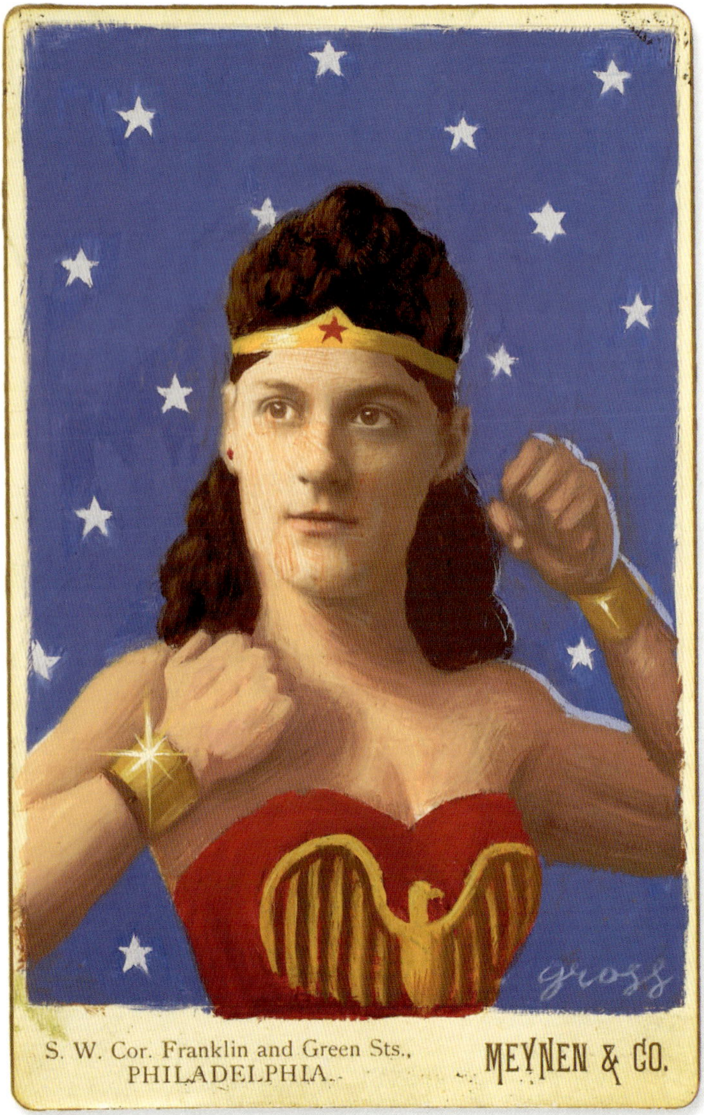
S. W. Cor. Franklin and Green Sts.,
PHILADELPHIA.
MEYNEN & CO.
gross

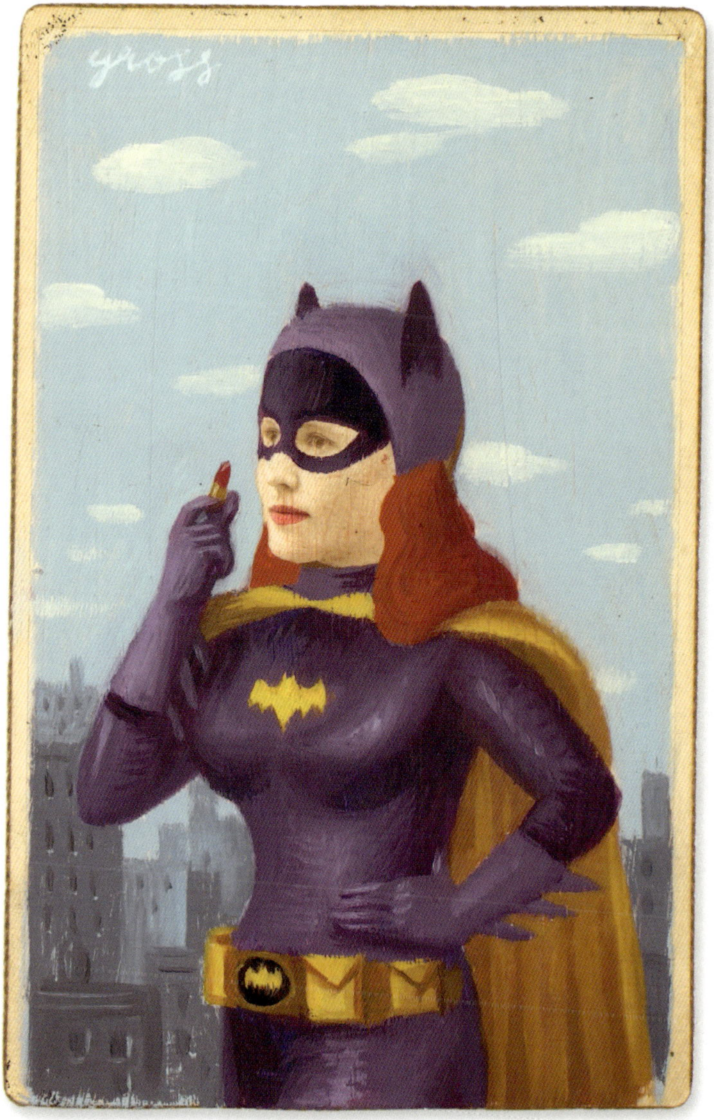
gross

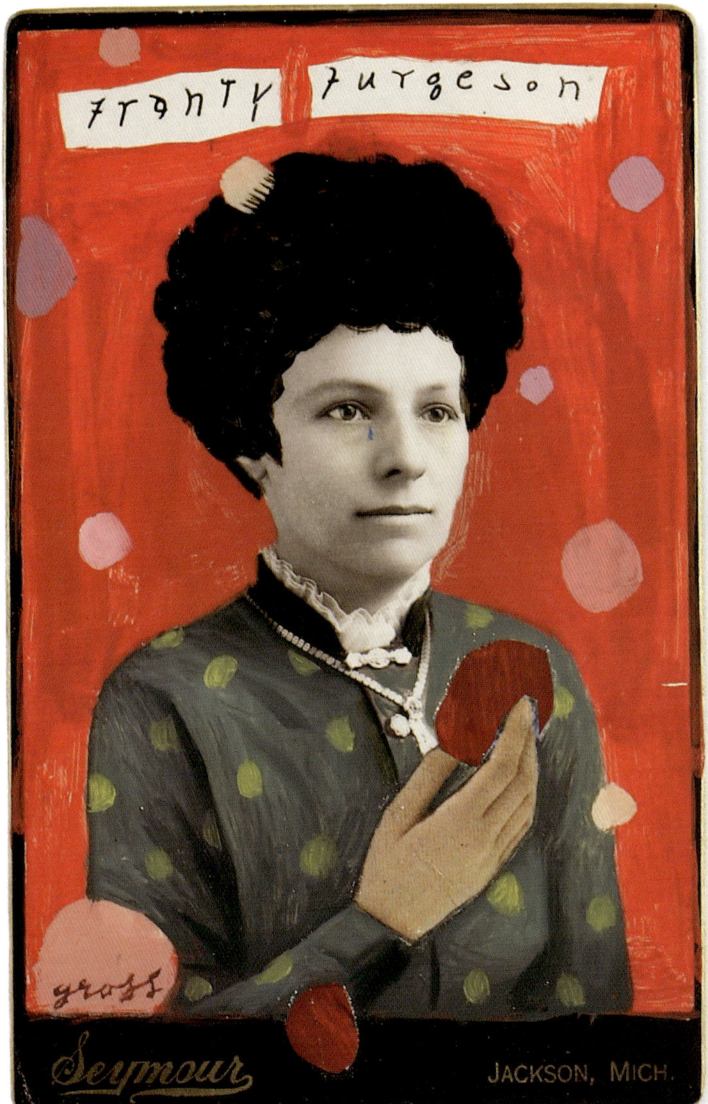
franty furgeson
gross
Seymour
JACKSON, MICH.

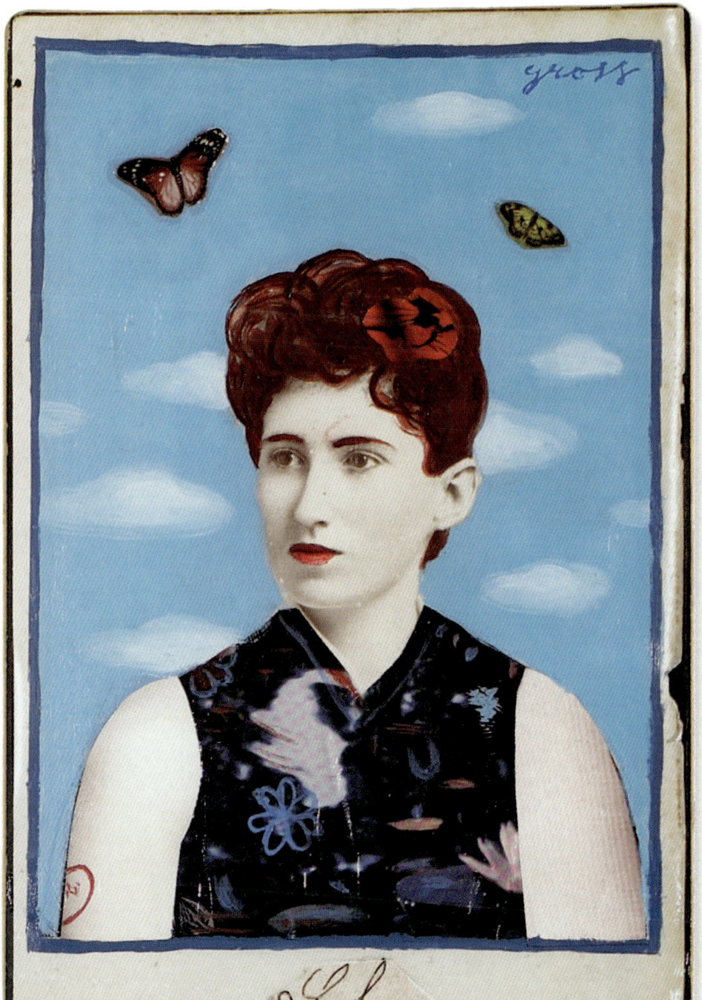
gross
Lola.
WATSON,
Raleigh, N. C.

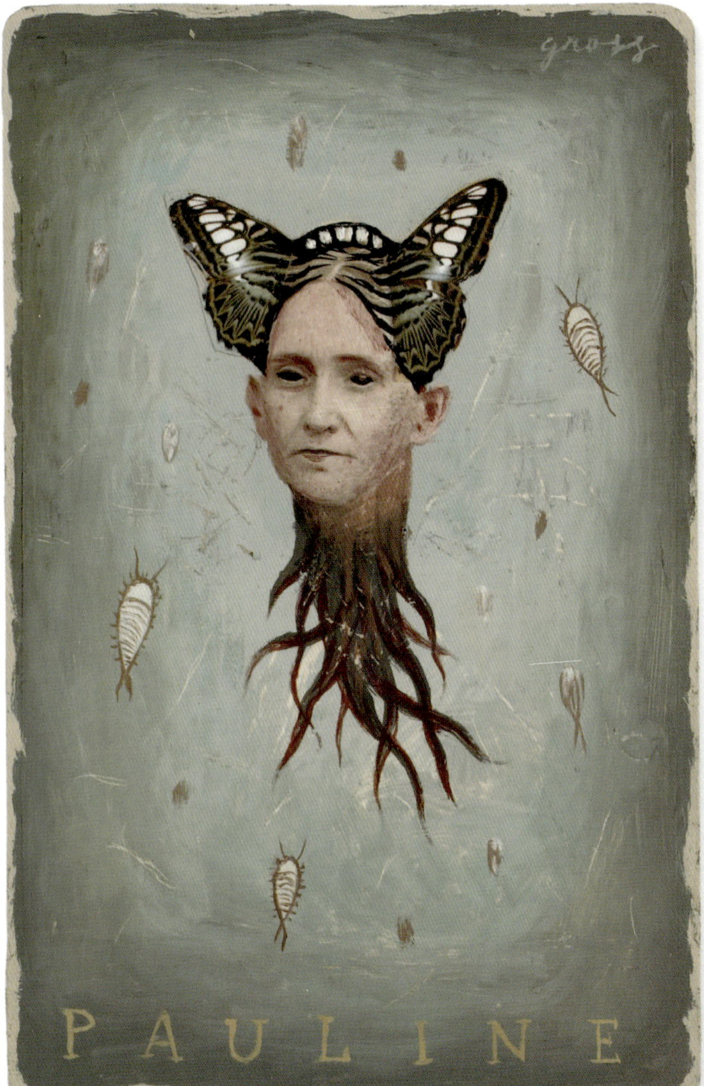
gross
PAULINE

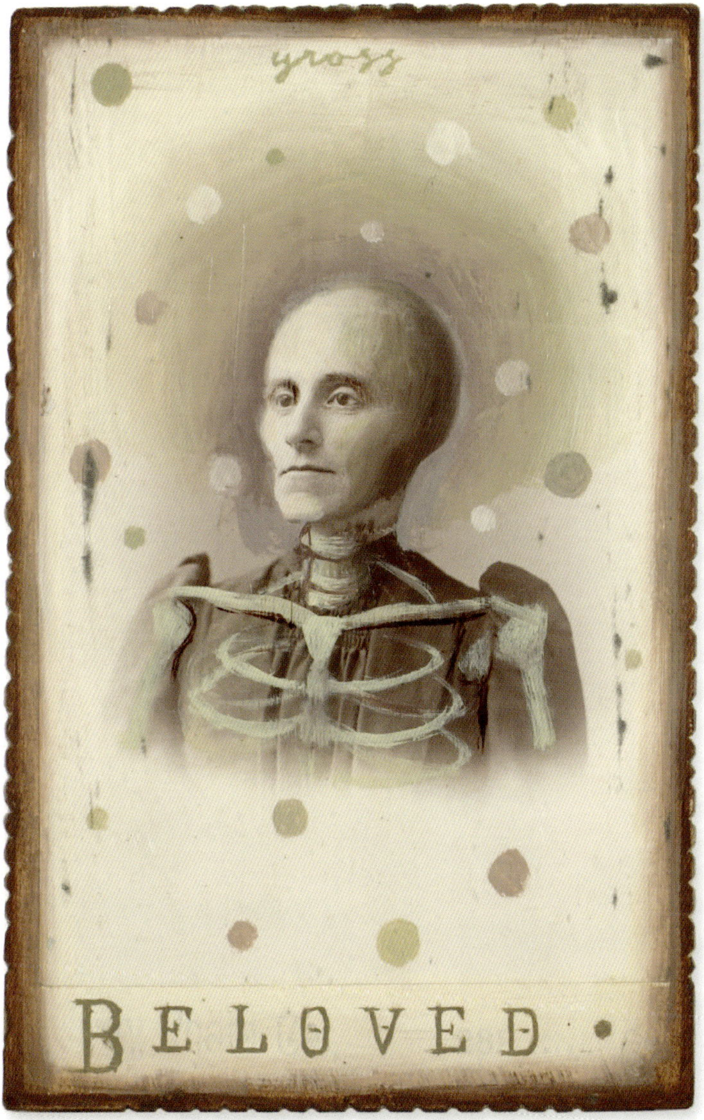
gross
BELOVED

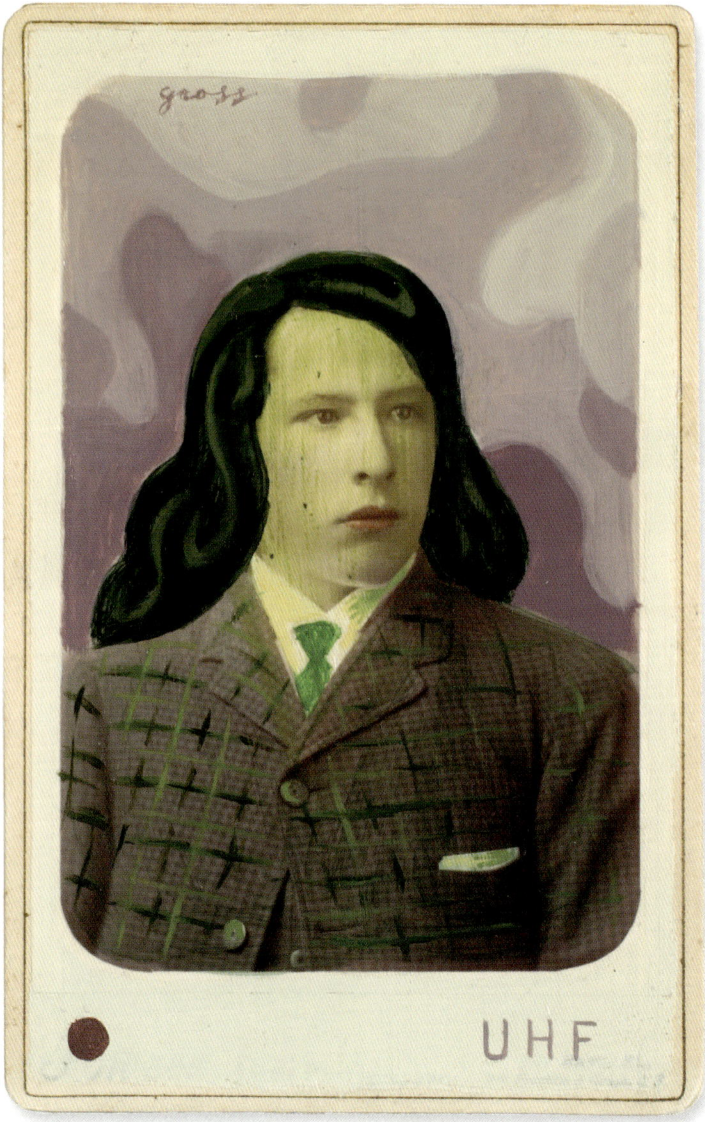
gross
UHF

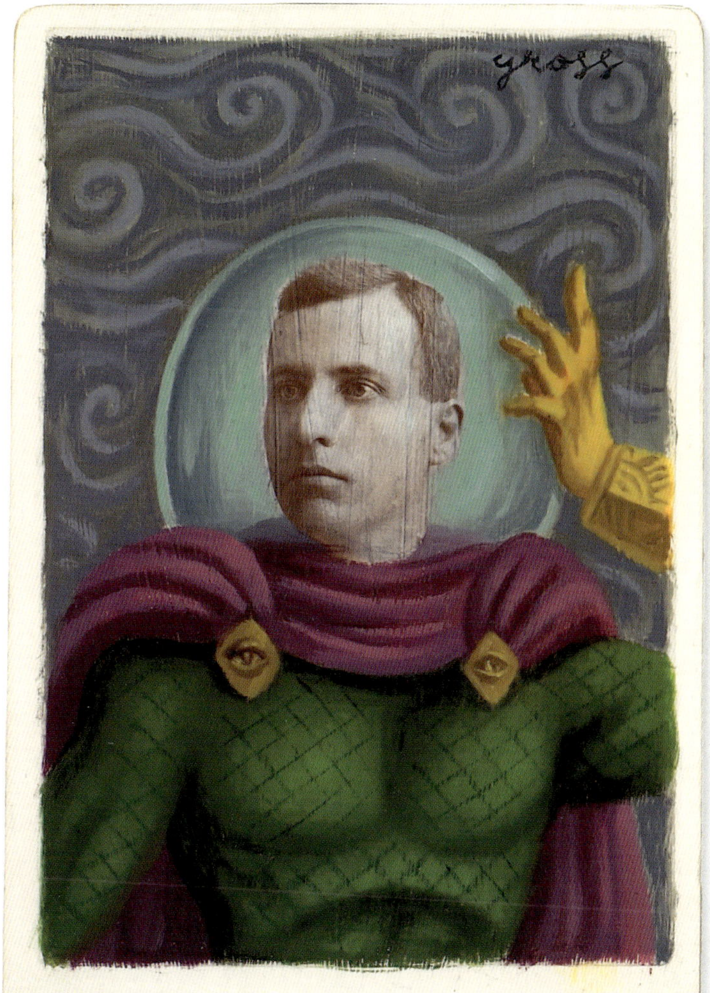
gross
Sunbeam Studio
78 Oregon St.
OSHKOSH.

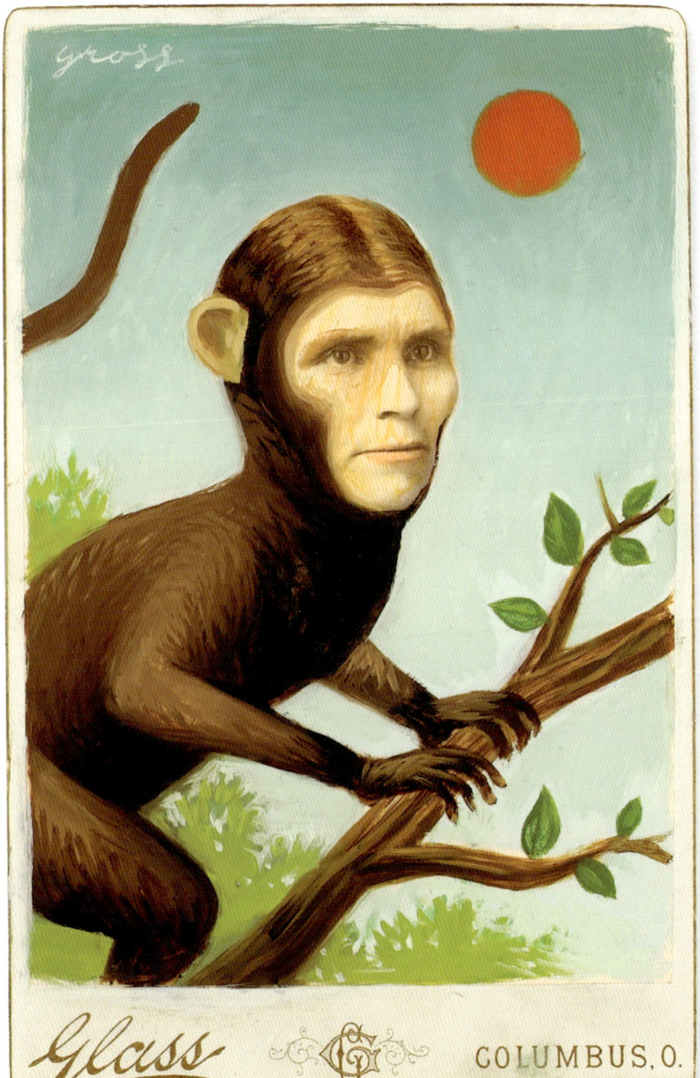
Gross
Glass
G
COLUMBUS, O.

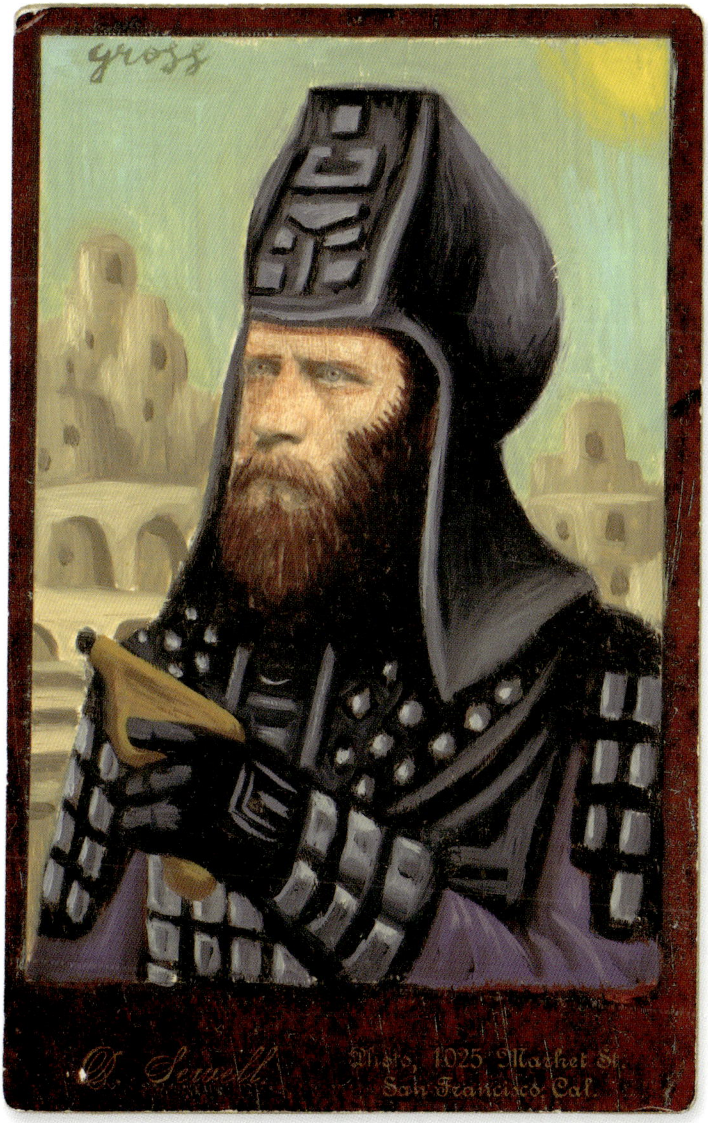
gross
Sewell
1025 Market St.
San Francisco, Cal.

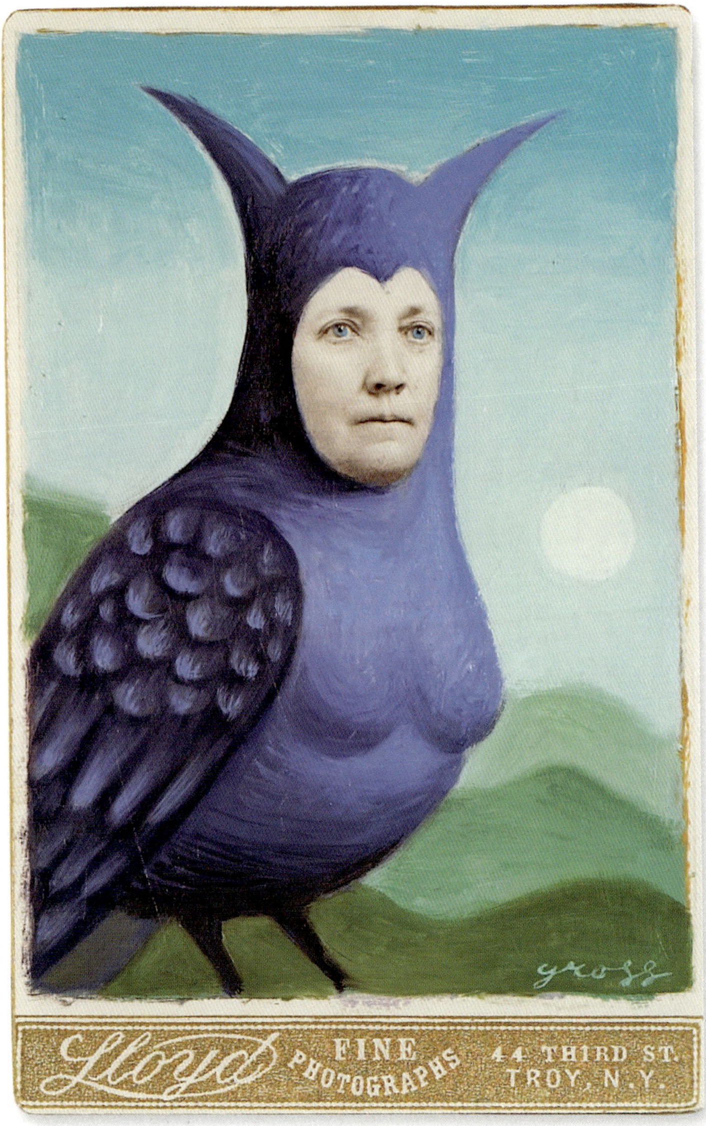
gross
Lloyd
FINE
PHOTOGRAPHS
44 THIRD ST.
TROY, N.Y.

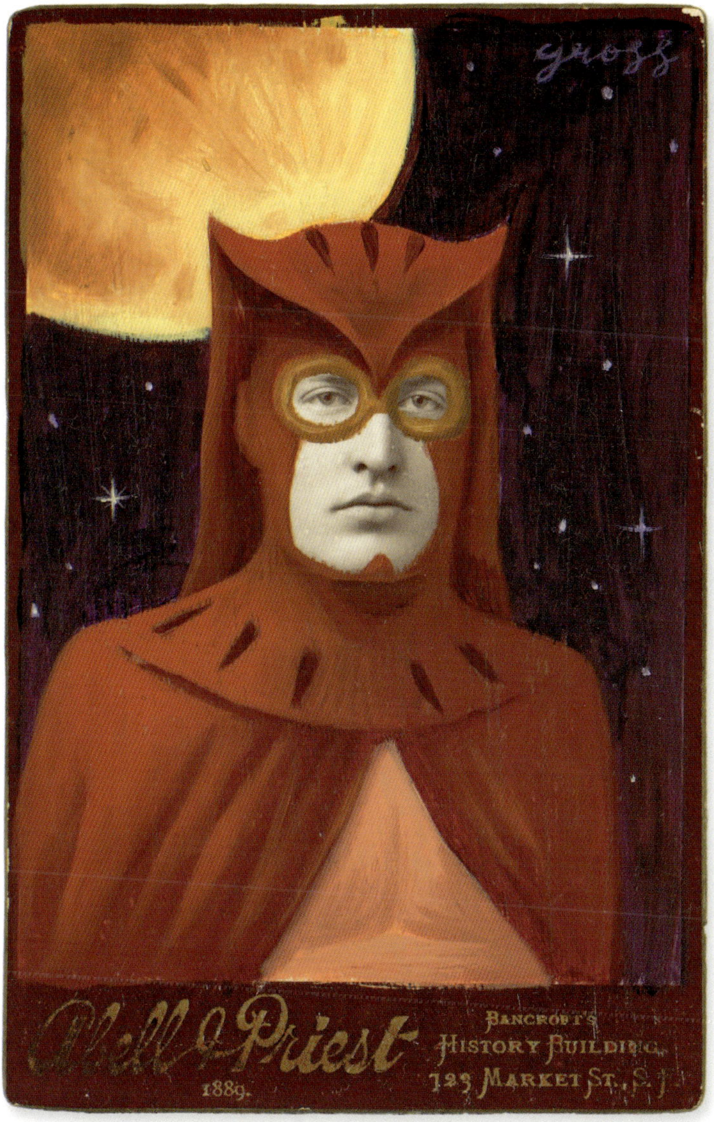
gross
Bancroft's
History Building.
123 Market St., S. F.
1889.

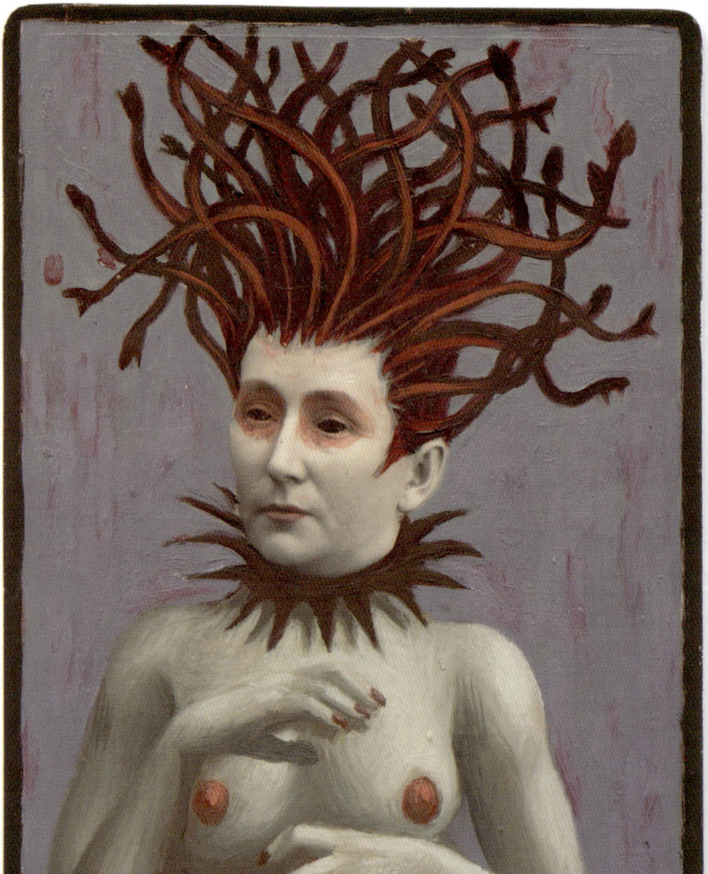
gross

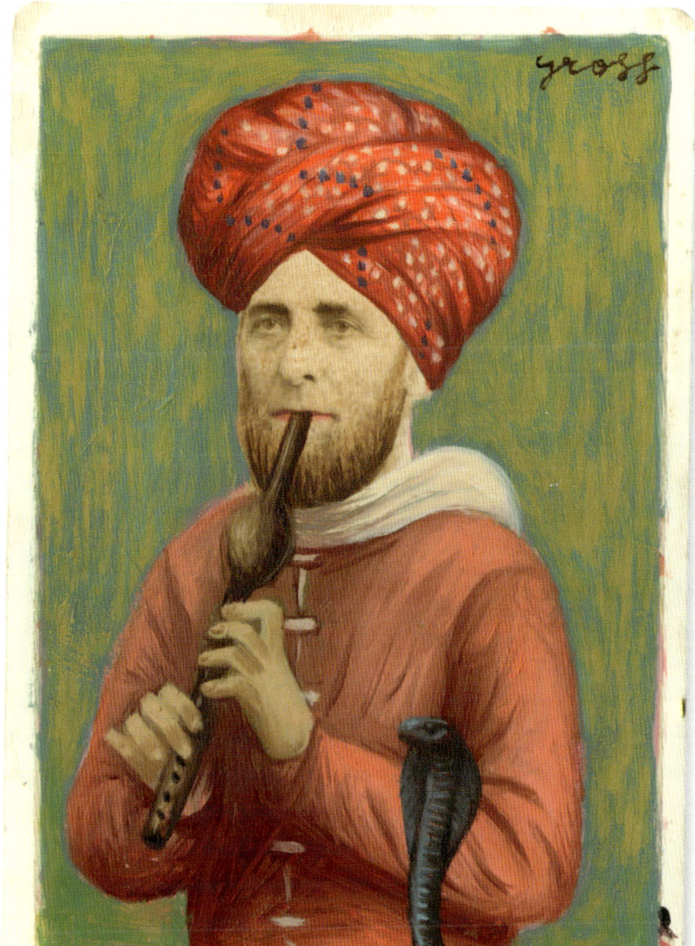
gross
914 MARKET ST.
SAN FRANCISCO.

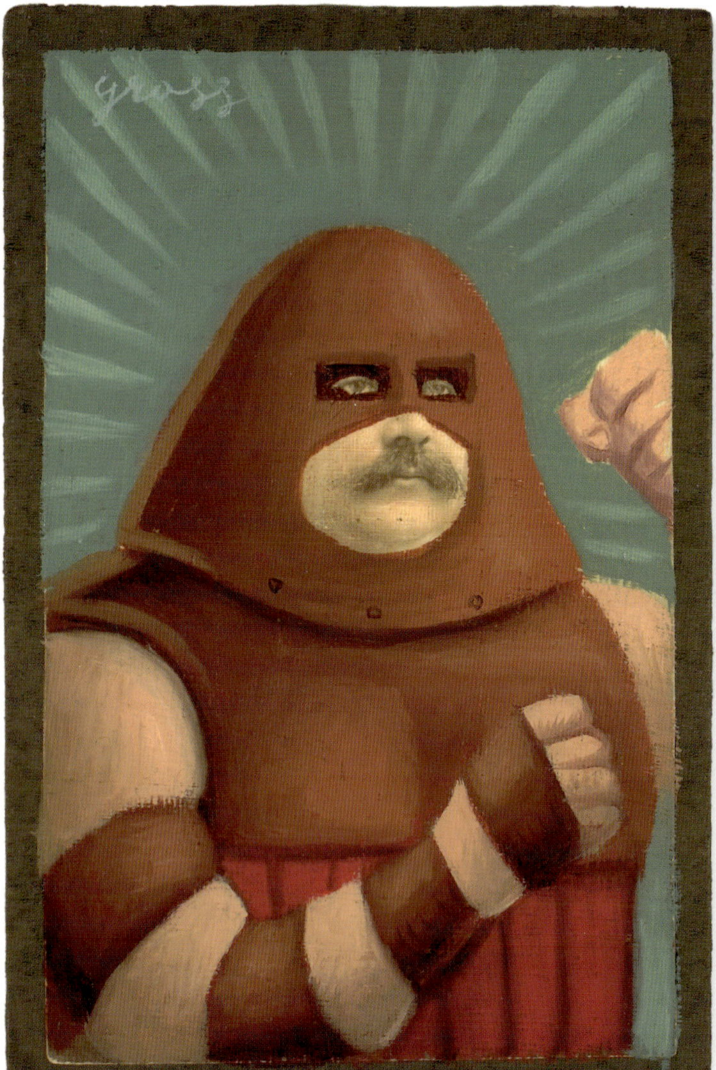

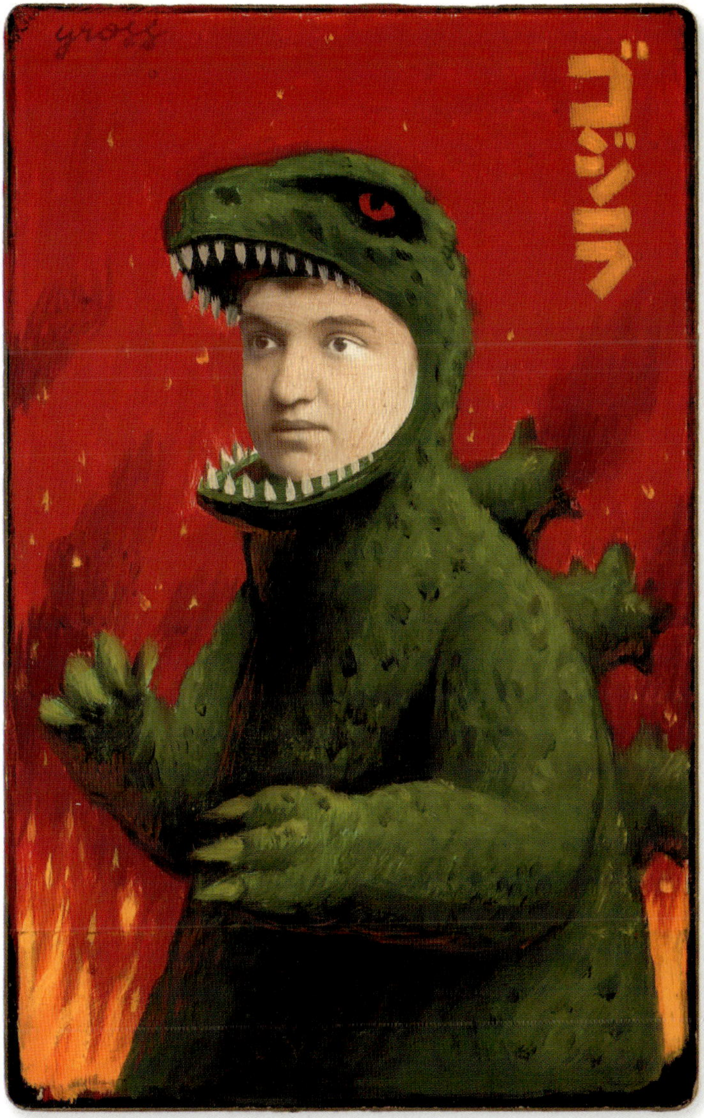
ゴジラ

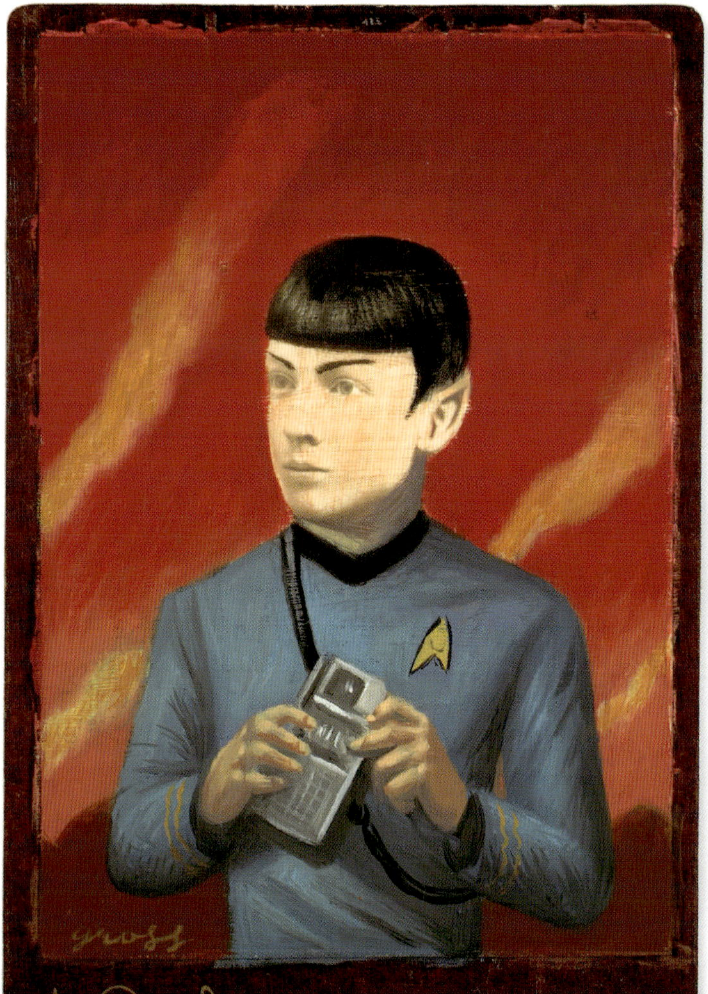
grogs
Kirchner
2198 THIRD AVENUE,
NEW YORK.
Entrance on 120th Street.

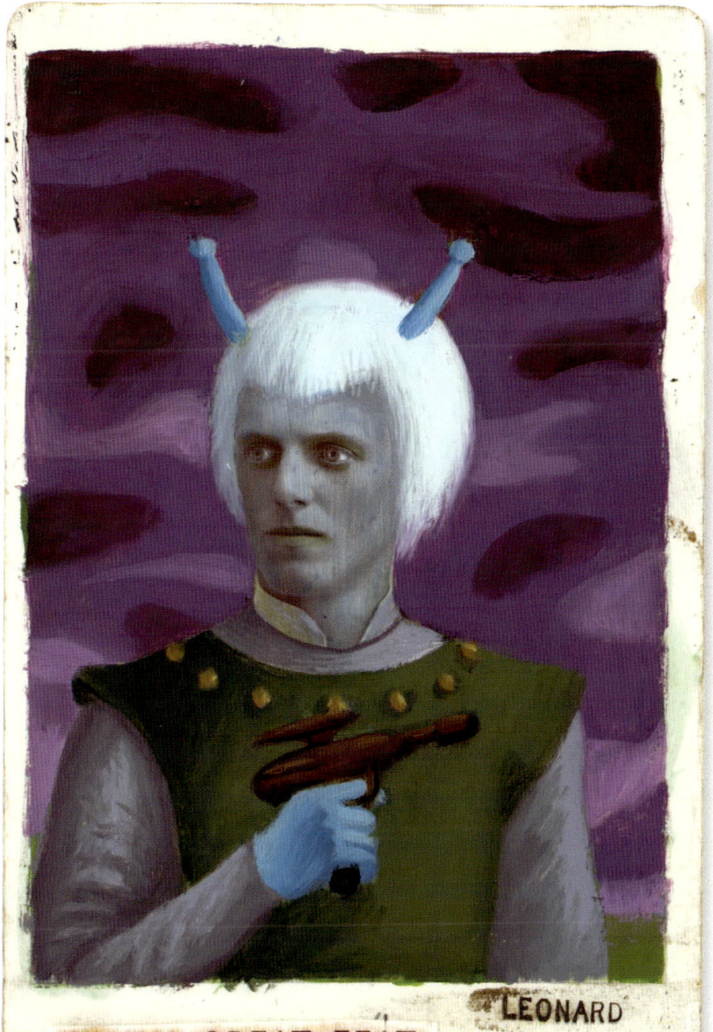
LEONARD
IN HIS GREAT FEAT,

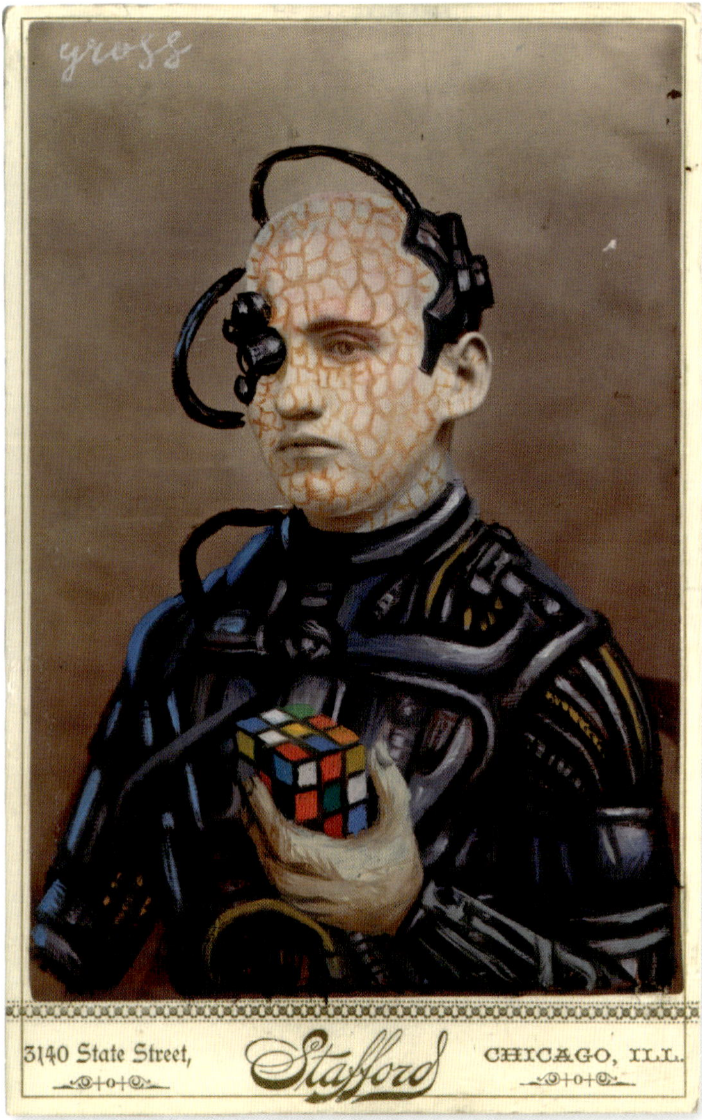
gross
3140 State Street,
Stafford
CHICAGO, ILL.

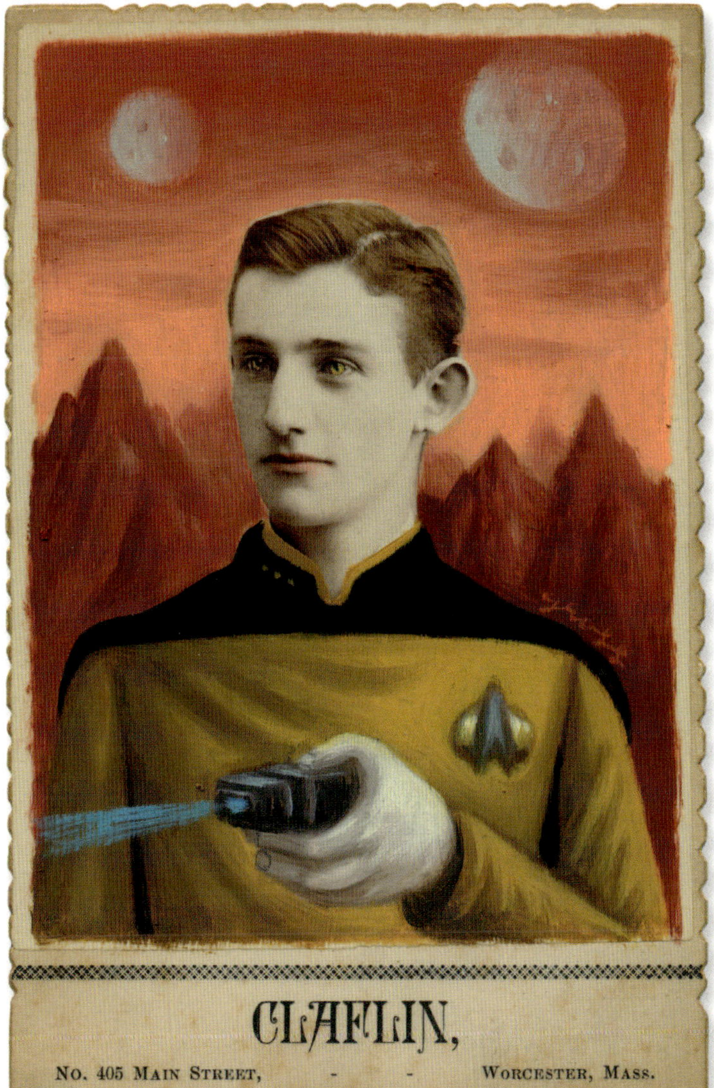
CLAFLIN,
No. 405 Main Street, - - Worcester, Mass.

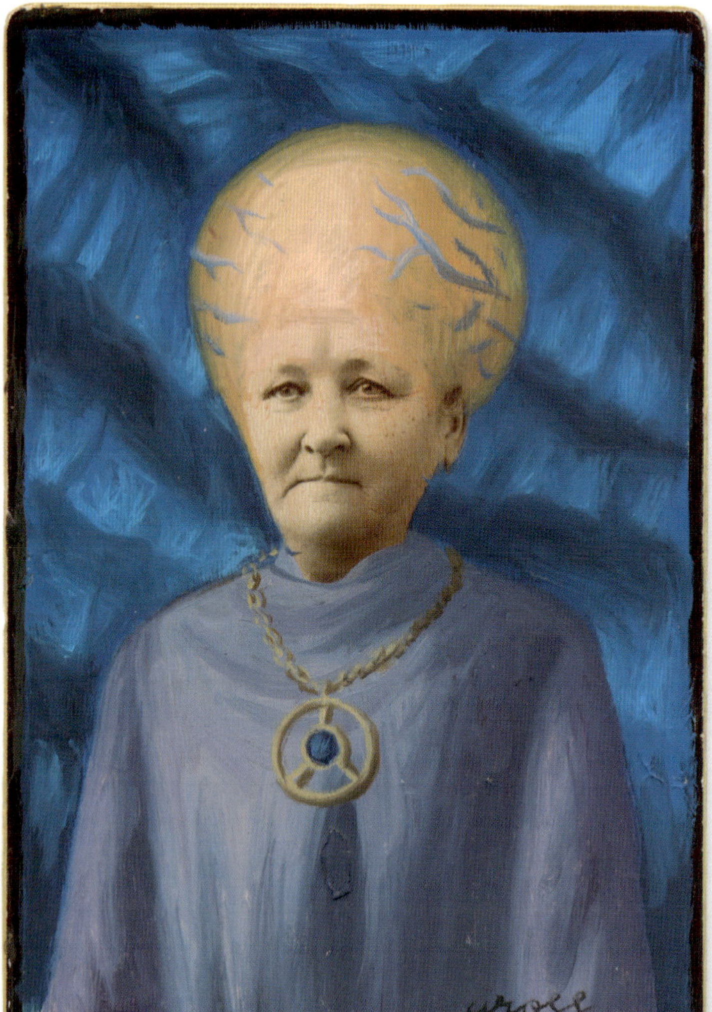
gross
R. H. FURMAN, - - CORONADO, CAL.

"Before" Images

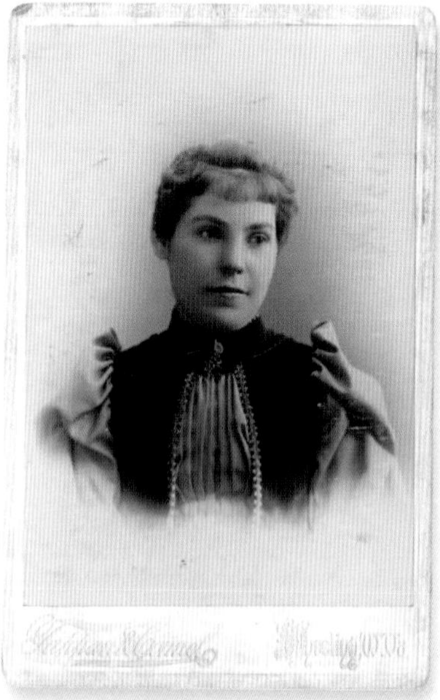

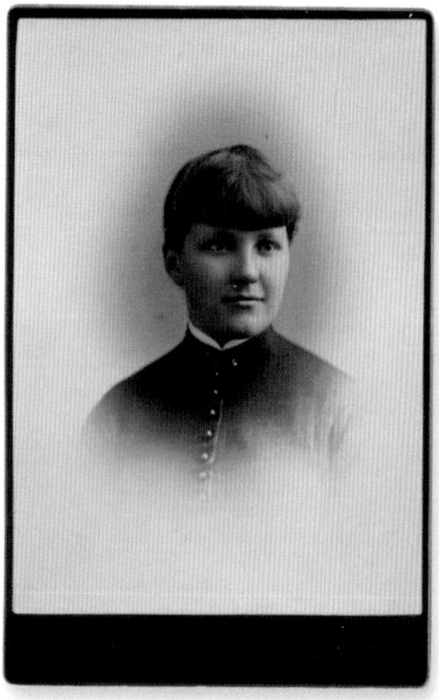

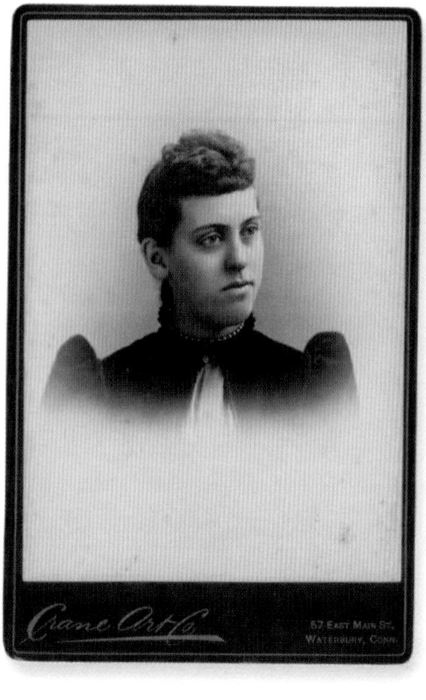
Crane Art Co.
57 East Main St.
Waterbury, Conn.

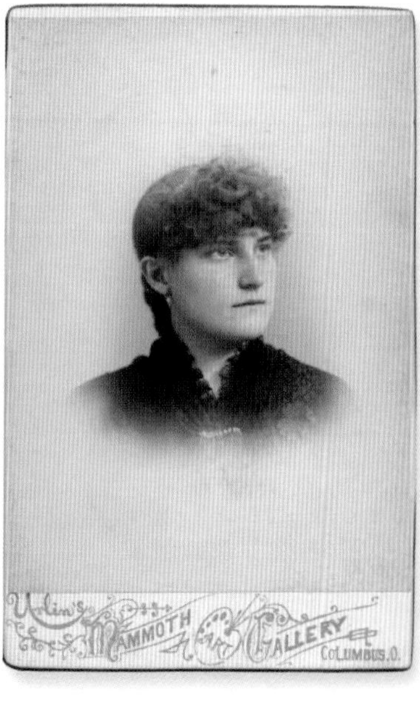
Urlin's
MAMMOTH
GALLERY
COLUMBUS, O.

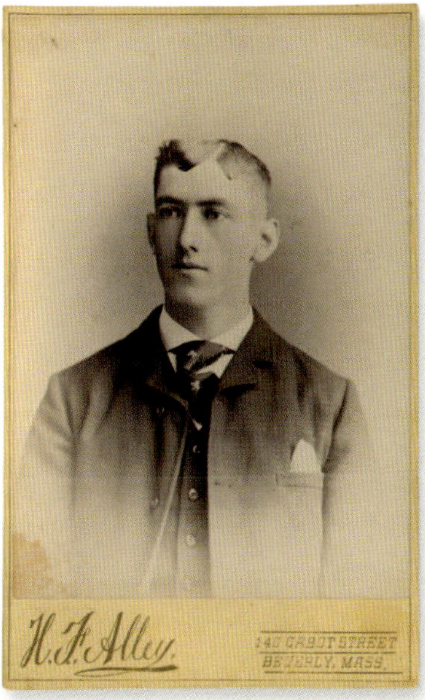
H. F. Alley
140 CABOT STREET
BEVERLY, MASS.

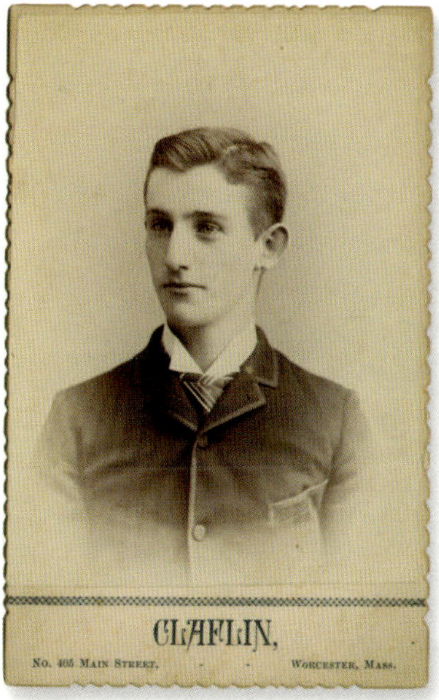
CLAFLIN,
No. 405 Main Street, Worcester, Mass.

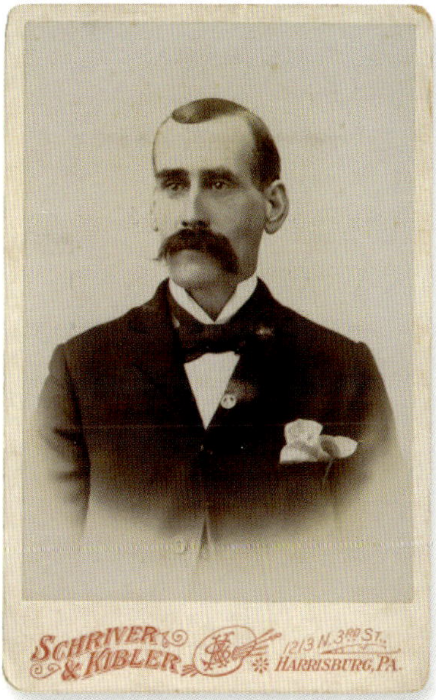
Schriver & Kibler
1213 N. 3rd St.
Harrisburg, Pa.

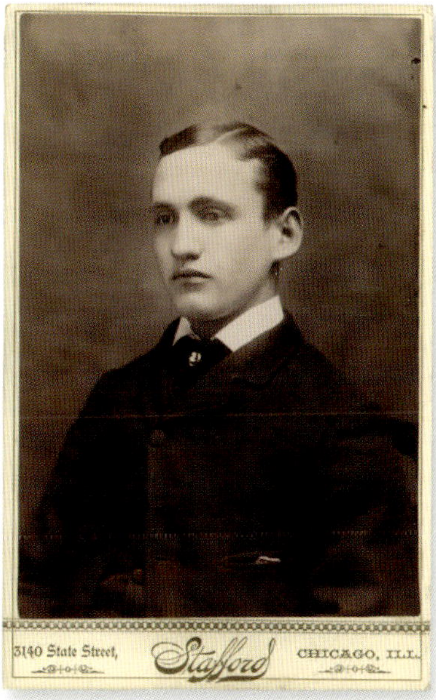
3140 State Street,
Stafford
CHICAGO, ILL.

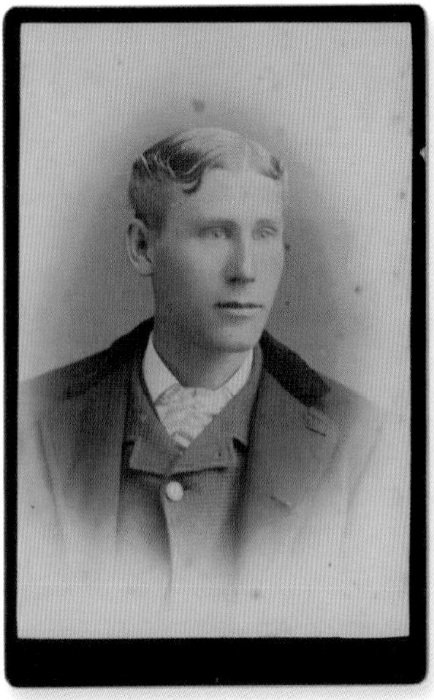

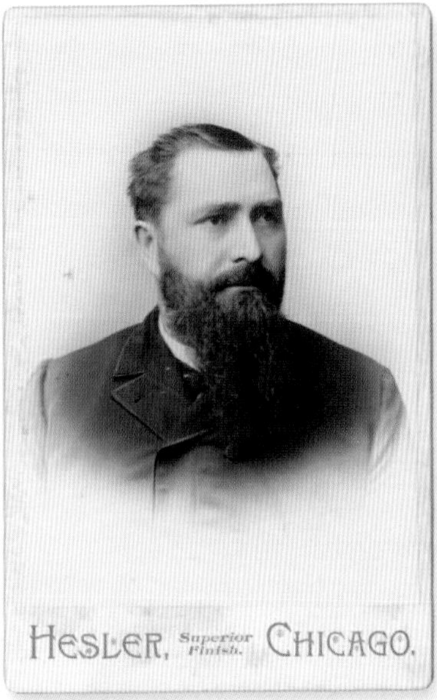
HESLER, Superior Finish. CHICAGO.

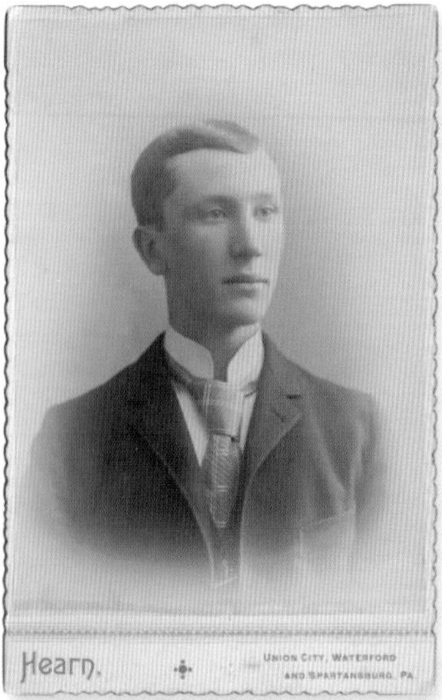
Hearn,
UNION CITY, WATERFORD
AND SPARTANSBURG, PA.

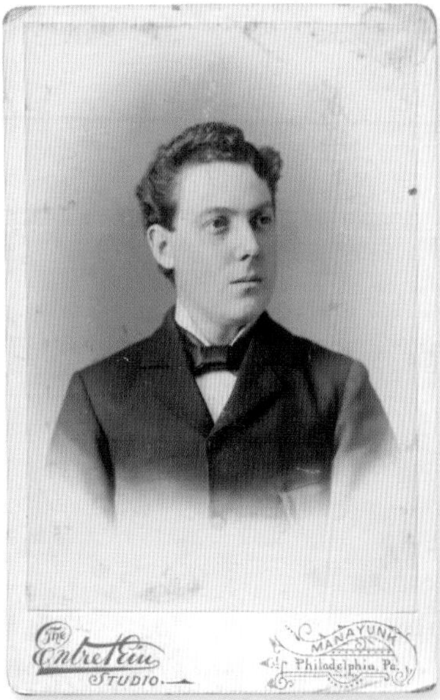
MANAYUNK
Philadelphia, Pa.

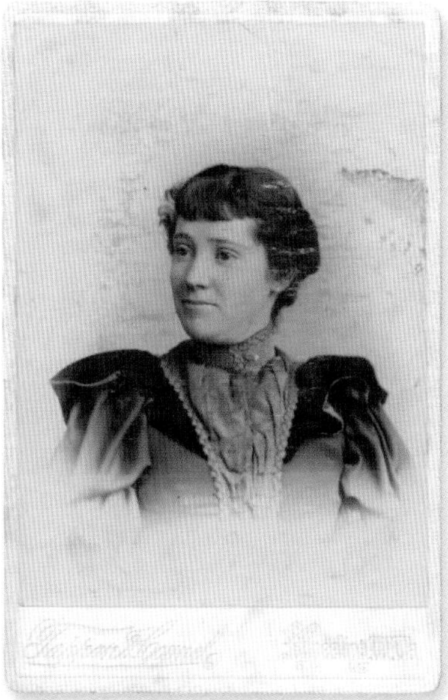

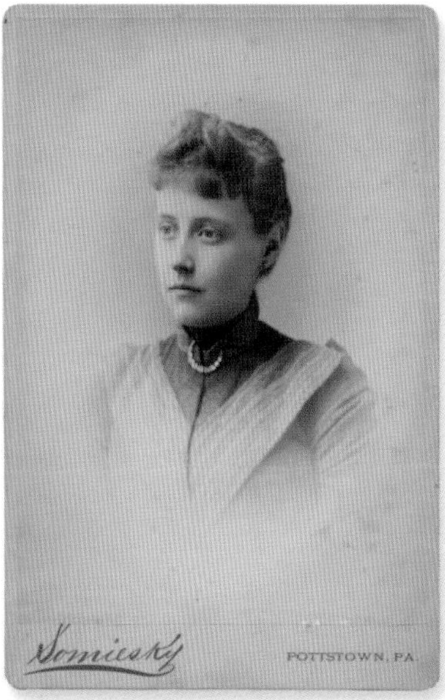
Somiesky
POTTSTOWN, PA.

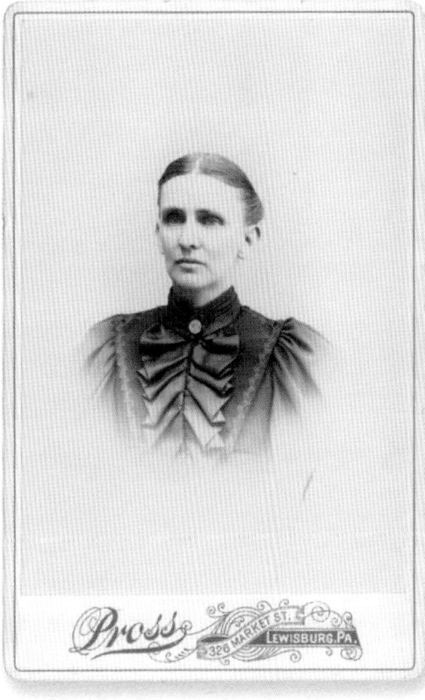
Pross
326 MARKET ST.
LEWISBURG, PA.

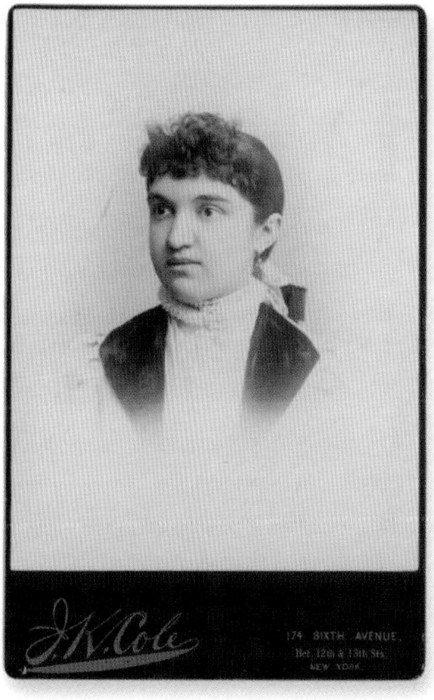
J.K. Cole
174 SIXTH AVENUE
Bet. 12th & 13th Sts.
NEW YORK

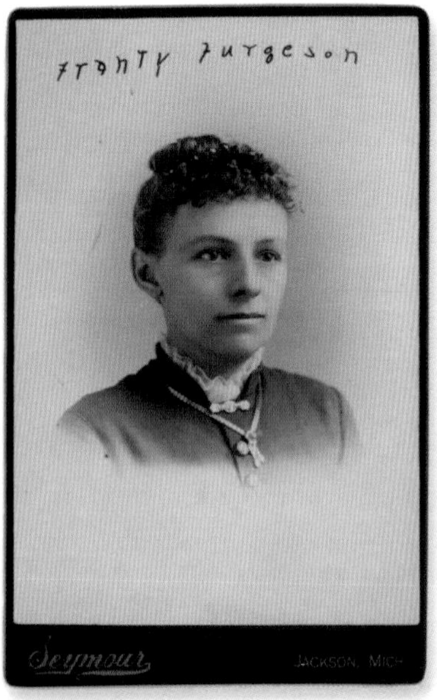
Franty Jurgeson
Seymour
JACKSON, MICH

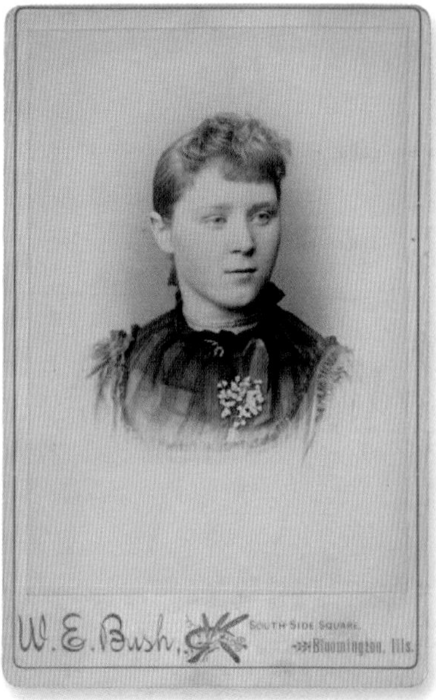
W. E. Bush,
SOUTH SIDE SQUARE,
Bloomington, Ills.

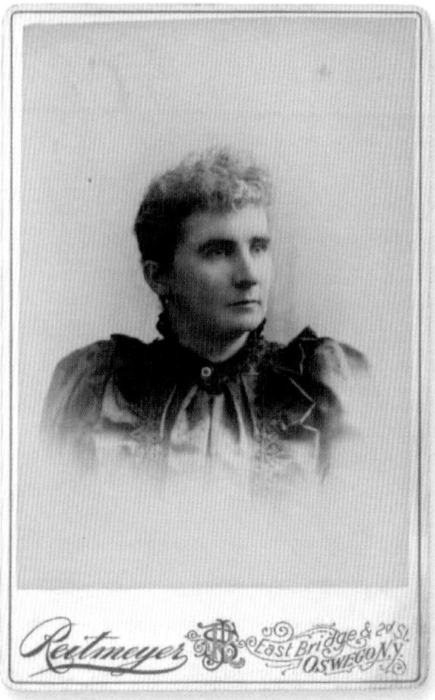
Reitmeyer
East Bridge & 2d St.
OSWEGO, N.Y.

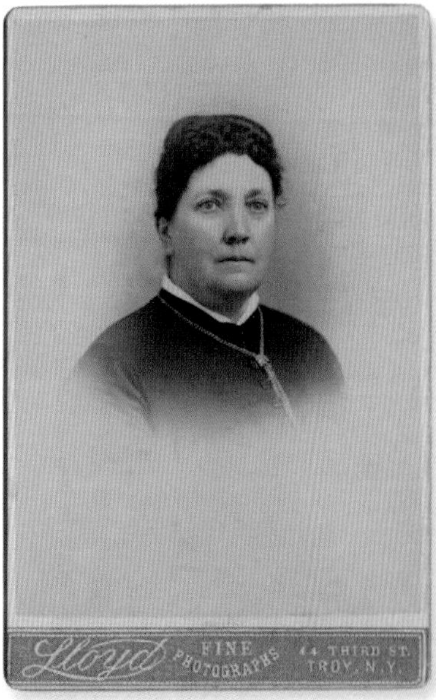
Lloyd
FINE PHOTOGRAPHS
44 THIRD ST.
TROY, N.Y.

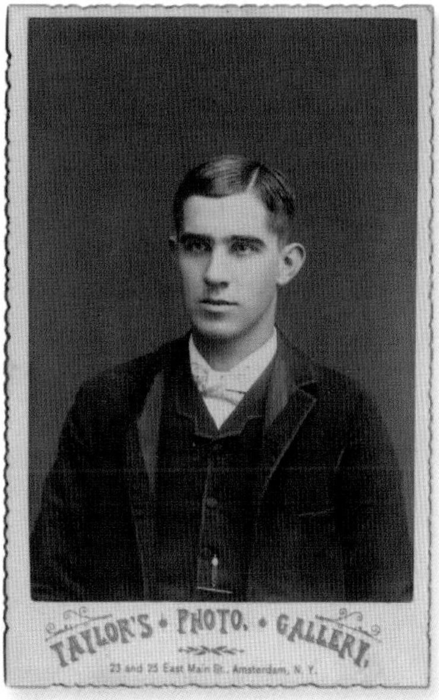
TAYLOR'S • PHOTO. • GALLERY.
23 and 25 East Main St., Amsterdam, N.Y.

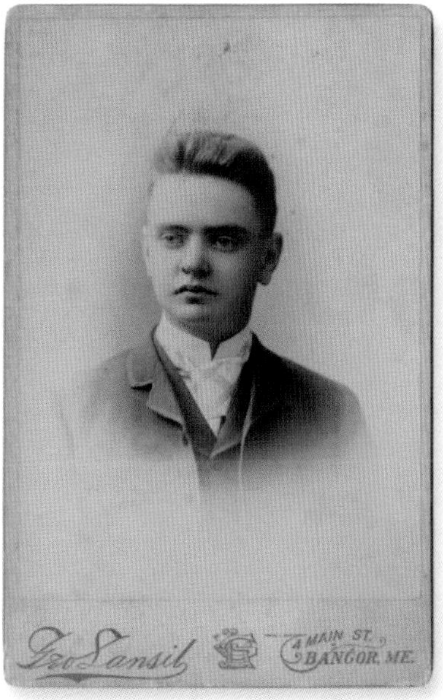
Geo Lansil
4 MAIN ST.
BANGOR, ME.

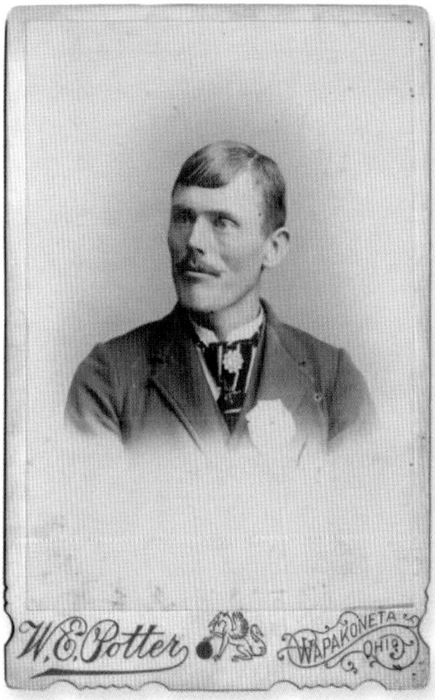
W.E. Potter
WAPAKONETA
OHIO

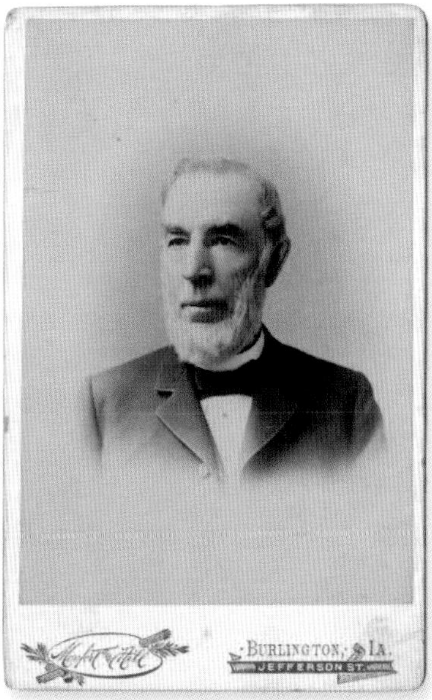
BURLINGTON, IA.
JEFFERSON ST.

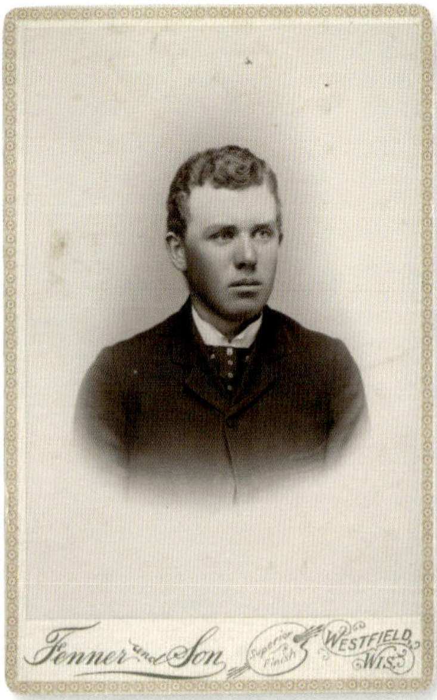
Fenner and Son
Superior Finish
WESTFIELD, WIS.

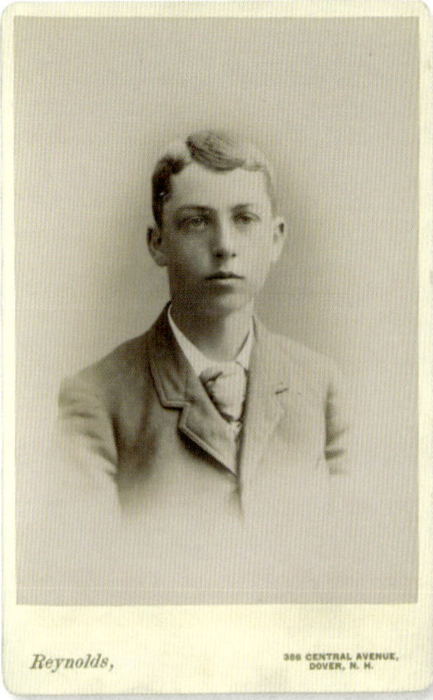
Reynolds,
386 CENTRAL AVENUE,
DOVER, N. H.

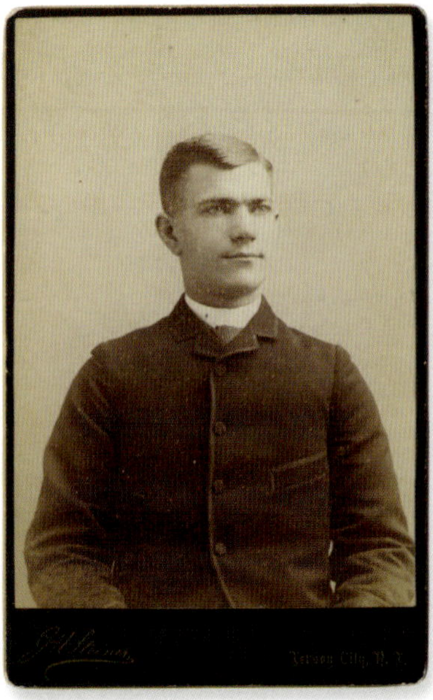

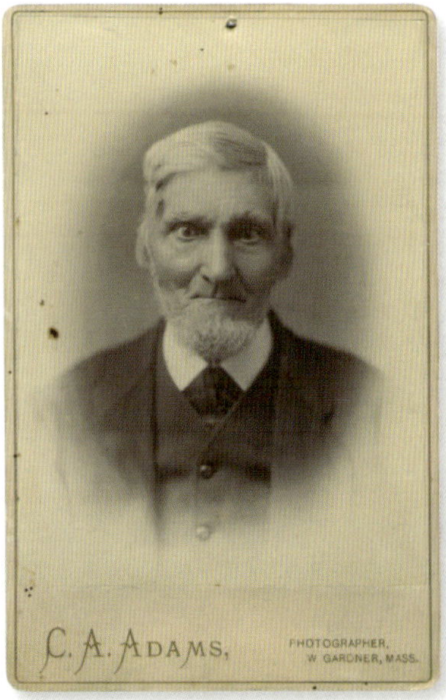
C. A. ADAMS,
PHOTOGRAPHER,
W. GARDNER, MASS.

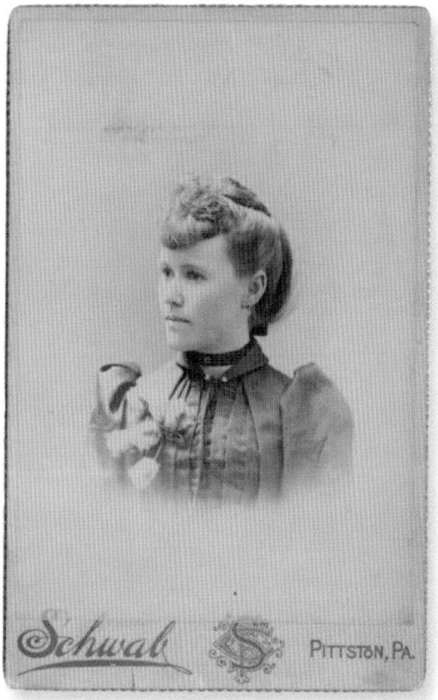
Schwab
PITTSTON, PA.

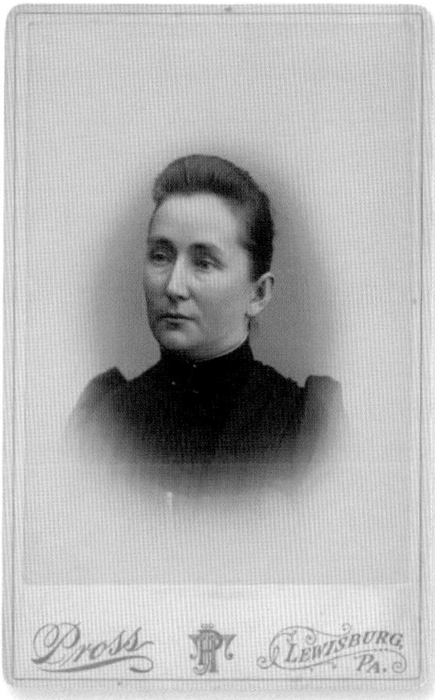
Pross
LEWISBURG, PA.

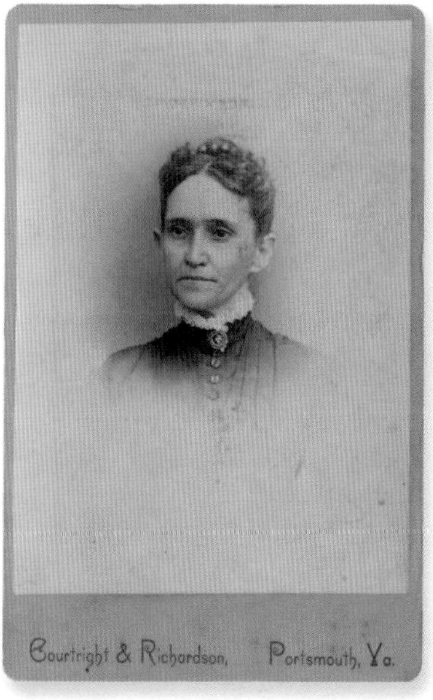
Courtright & Richardson,
Portsmouth, Va.

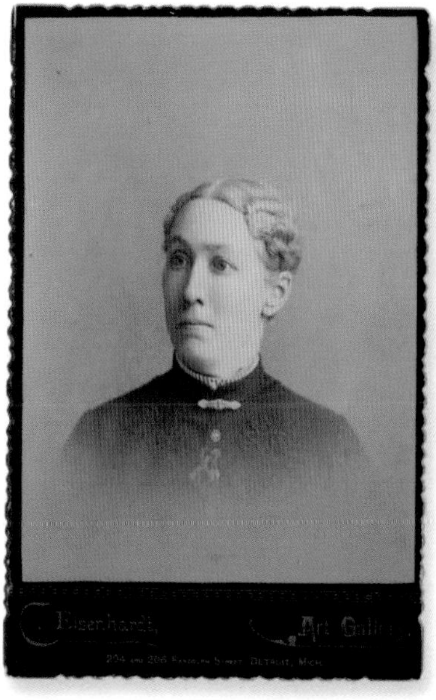
Eisenhardt,

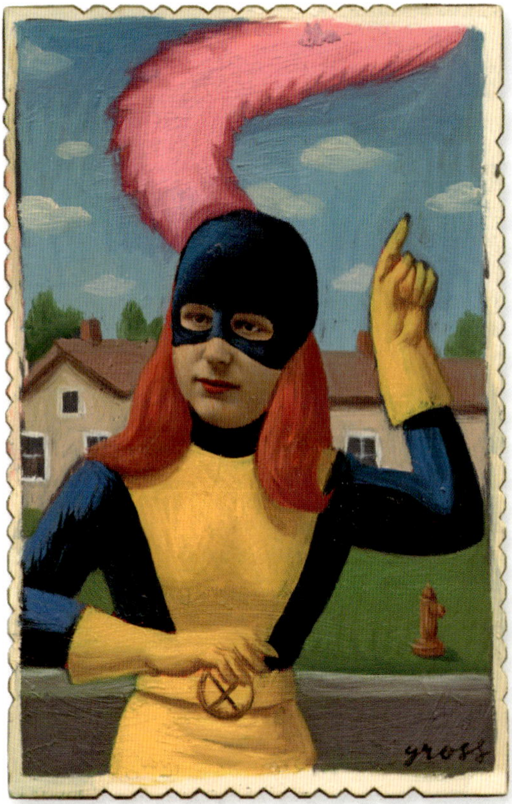

First Published in the United States of America, February, 2012

Second Printing

Gingko Press, Inc. - 1321 Fifth Street - Berkeley, CA 94710, USA

Phone (510) 898 1195 - email: books@gingkopress.com - www.gingkopress.com

ISBN: 978-1-58423-487-6

Printed in China

Designed by Alex Gross and Cindy Vance

© 2012 Alex Gross all artwork

All Rights Reserved.

No part of this book may be reproduced or utilized in any form or by any means, mechanical or electronic, including, but not limited to photocopying, scanning and recording by any information and retrieval system, without permission in writing from the publisher.

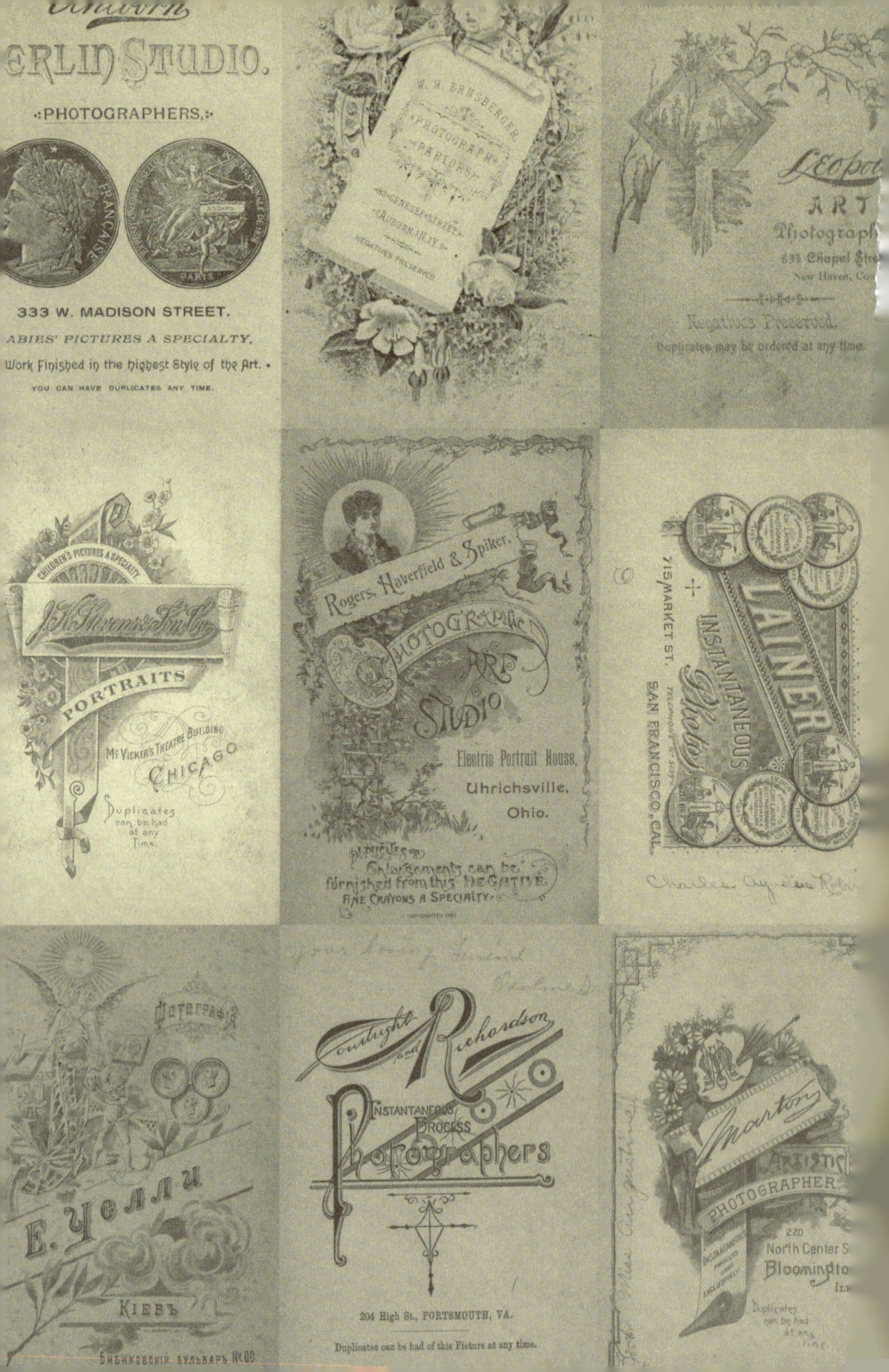
ERLIN STUDIO.
PHOTOGRAPHERS,
FRANCAISE
PARIS
333 W. MADISON STREET.
ABIES' PICTURES A SPECIALTY.
Work Finished in the highest Style of the Art.
YOU CAN HAVE DUPLICATES ANY TIME.
W. H. ERNSBERGER
PHOTOGRAPH PARLORS
GENESEE STREET
AUBURN, N.Y.
NEGATIVES PRESERVED
ART
Photograph
Chapel Stre
New Haven, Co
Negatives Preserved.
Duplicates may be ordered at any time.
CHILDREN'S PICTURES A SPECIALTY
J. K. Stevens & Son Co.
PORTRAITS
McVICKER'S THEATRE BUILDING
CHICAGO
Duplicates can be had at any Time.
Rogers, Haverfield & Spiker,
PHOTOGRAPHIC
ART
STUDIO
Electric Portrait House,
Uhrichsville,
Ohio.
DUPLICATES OF
Enlargements can be furnished from this NEGATIVE
FINE CRAYONS A SPECIALTY
715 MARKET ST.
LAINER
INSTANTANEOUS
Photos
SAN FRANCISCO, CAL.
Фотографiя
Е. Челли
КIЕВЪ
Cartright and Richardson
INSTANTANEOUS PROCESS
Photographers
204 High St., PORTSMOUTH, VA.
Duplicates can be had of this Picture at any time.
Marton
ARTISTIC
PHOTOGRAPHER
INSTANTANEOUS PROCESS USED EXCLUSIVELY
220
North Center S
Blooming
Duplicates can be had at any time